The Economics of Food

How Feeding and Fueling the Planet Affects Food Prices

Patrick Westhoff

Vice President, Publisher: Tim Moore
Associate Publisher and Director of Marketing: Amy Neidlinger
Executive Editor: Jim Boyd
Editorial Assistants: Pamela Boland, Myesha Graham
Development Editor: Russ Hall
Operations Manager: Gina Kanouse
Senior Marketing Manager: Julie Phifer
Publicity Manager: Laura Czaja
Assistant Marketing Manager: Megan Colvin
Cover Designer: Alan Clements
Managing Editor: Kristy Hart
Project Editor: Betsy Harris
Copy Editor: Keith Cline
Proofreader: Dan Knott
Senior Indexer: Cheryl Lenser
Compositor: Jake McFarland
Manufacturing Buyer: Dan Uhrig

FT Press offers excellent discounts on this book when ordered in quantity for bulk purchases or special sales. For more information, please contact U.S. Corporate and Government Sales, 1-800-382-3419, corpsales@pearsontechgroup.com. For sales outside the U.S., please contact International Sales at international@pearson.com.

First Printing March 2010

ISBN-10: 0-13-700610-1
ISBN-13: 978-0-13-700610-6

Pearson Education LTD.
Pearson Education Australia PTY, Limited.
Pearson Education Singapore, Pte. Ltd.
Pearson Education North Asia, Ltd.
Pearson Education Canada, Ltd.
Pearson Educatión de Mexico, S.A. de C.V.
Pearson Education—Japan
Pearson Education Malaysia, Pte. Ltd.

Library of Congress Cataloging-in-Publication Data
Westhoff, Patrick C. (Patrick Charles), 1958-
    The economics of food : how feeding and fueling the planet affects food prices / Patrick Westhoff.
       p. cm.
Includes bibliographical references.
ISBN-13: 978-0-13-700610-6 (hardback : alk. paper)
ISBN-10: 0-13-700610-1 (hardback : alk. paper) 1. Food prices. 2. Biomass energy. 3. Agriculture--Economic aspects. I. Title.
   HD9000.4.W47 2010
   338.1'9--dc22
                                                            2009042440

In memory of Trisha Westhoff Yauk.
We miss you, Sis.

Contents

Acknowledgments

Many people made this book possible. Editor Jim Boyd first contacted me about the idea of writing a book concerning the world food crisis. Without his guidance and patience, this book would never have been completed. I have been very fortunate to work with him and the entire team at Pearson.

This work grew out of my work with the Food and Agricultural Policy Research Institute (FAPRI) at the University of Missouri. Willi Meyers, Abner Womack, Scott Brown, Lori Wilcox, Wyatt Thompson, Seth Meyer, Julian Binfield, and the rest of the FAPRI staff provided most of the good ideas and gave me the time I needed to work on the project.

Colleagues at Iowa State University, Texas A&M University, the U.S. Department of Agriculture, the Congressional Budget Office, the Organization for Economic Cooperation and Development, the U.N. Food and Agriculture Organization, and FAPRI-affiliated institutions in Ireland, the United Kingdom, South Africa, South Korea, and Mexico helped to shape my thinking about food markets. Michael Thomsett and Greg Karp offered very helpful comments and suggestions on an earlier draft.

Although many people contributed to this book, none of them are responsible for the remaining errors. All opinions expressed are mine, and not necessarily those of FAPRI or the University of Missouri.

Finally, special thanks to my family. This book could not have been written without the love and support of my wife, Elena, and our children, Christina, Ben, and Maria.

About the Author

Patrick Westhoff grew up on a small dairy farm in Iowa, just a few miles from the "Field of Dreams." He earned an undergraduate degree in political science from the University of Iowa and then spent two years in the Peace Corps in Guatemala, working with small-scale farmers. After getting a master's degree in Latin American studies from the University of Texas, he moved back to Iowa and earned a Ph.D. in agricultural economics from Iowa State University in 1989.

From 1992–1996, he served as an economist with the U.S. Senate Committee on Agriculture, Nutrition, and Forestry. He worked on several major pieces of legislation, including the 1996 farm bill.

Westhoff has spent most of his professional career studying agricultural markets and policies with the Food and Agricultural Policy Research Institute (FAPRI), first at Iowa State University and now at the University of Missouri. FAPRI analysis is used by the U.S. Congress, the United Nation's Food and Agriculture Organization (FAO), the Organization for Economic Cooperation and Development (OECD), and national institutions in Europe, Asia, Africa, and Latin America. In November 2007, he was named a co-director of the FAPRI unit at the University of Missouri (MU). The author also teaches and advises graduate students in the MU Department of Agricultural Economics.

Introduction: What Goes Up...

Everyone eats, and billions of people around the world work in agriculture and related industries. Food prices are important to everyone and literally a matter of life and death for some.

The prices we pay at the grocery store depend on everything from the weather in Iowa and India to the types of fuel we put in our cars in London and Los Angeles. Economic growth in China affects the price of a pizza in Chicago. Understanding why food prices rise and fall can help us anticipate and react to future market developments. It can also help us make important decisions as a society about how best to feed and fuel the planet.

For many years, food prices did not get a lot of attention. From 1991 to 2006, U.S. consumer food prices increased just 2.5 percent per year, slightly less than the overall inflation rate.[1] Crop and livestock prices varied from year to year, but with little overall trend.

Food prices got a lot of attention in 2007 and 2008. Front-page stories highlighted a sudden rise in food prices and a December 2007 cover story in *The Economist* proclaimed "The End of Cheap Food." U.S. consumer food prices rose 4 percent in 2007, the largest increase since 1990, and the rate of food price inflation jumped to 5.5 percent in 2008. The surge in prices of basic staples was even more dramatic. Corn prices more than tripled between the fall of 2005 and the summer of 2008.[2] Prices for wheat, rice, soybeans, and many other staple foods also rose sharply.

The rise in food prices was a concern in the United States, but a crisis in much of the developing world. The average U.S. family of four spent $8,671 on food in 2007,[3] and rising food prices made it harder for families to make ends meet. In low-income countries, the average family may spend half or more of its income on food. Sharply

1

higher prices for staple foods meant low-income families were faced with a stark choice of eating less or cutting back on other necessities. The Food and Agriculture Organization estimates that millions of people were added to global hunger rolls in 2007 and 2008, leaving 915 million people undernourished. The world economic crisis could push that number over a billion in 2009.[4]

What goes up can come down. Just about the time many people became convinced that high food prices were here to stay, prices for grains and other crops retreated. Traders from around the world use futures markets to make or hedge bets about current and future prices for food and other products. Wheat futures prices reached record highs in March 2008, corn peaked in June, and soybeans in July. By late October 2008, wheat and corn futures had declined by more than 50 percent from the high, and soybean futures had dropped almost as much.[5] After peaking in June 2008, FAO's food price index fell by one-third over the next six months.[6] What happened? After years of stagnation, why did food prices suddenly explode and then collapse? Was this just a short-lived crisis, or are higher food prices and all their consequences likely to be the norm in the years ahead?

Journalists, policy makers, and economists have tried to explain the rapid changes in food prices. Some have provided well-reasoned analyses that carefully identify and weigh the many contributing factors. Others have tried to reduce the complex story to a sound bite, often to make a political point. A lot of information is available, but it is not easy to separate the information from the misinformation.

Increasing amounts of corn, sugar, vegetable oil, and animal fats are used to make ethanol and biodiesel, two biofuels that can be used to fuel cars and trucks. The role of biofuels in the increase in food prices has been especially controversial, and the debate has often generated more heat than light. Some have laid much or even most of the

2

blame for higher food prices on the growth in biofuel production in the United States and Europe. The more grain and vegetable oil is used to produce these biofuels, the less is available to feed people, biofuel opponents argue, and the losers in this food versus fuel battle have been food consumers around the world. Often quoted was a note by a World Bank economist that suggests the increase in biofuel production directly or indirectly accounted for 70 percent to 75 percent of the recent increase in food prices.[7]

On the other side of the argument, biofuel defenders point to a variety of benefits of the industry and contend that the role of biofuels in raising food prices is minimal. The share of the world's crops used to produce biofuels remains very small, they point out, and farmers around the world can and will increase production to satisfy the demand for both food and fuel. Former U.S. Secretary of Agriculture Ed Schafer frequently claimed that increased corn-based ethanol production only accounted for 3 percent of the increase in global food prices.[8] The actual impact of biofuels on food prices was almost certainly greater than biofuel proponents would like to acknowledge, but less than biofuel opponents claim.

This book makes sense of the various arguments about recent swings in food prices. Was the run-up in food prices a fluke, or a sign of things to come? Understanding what happened and why may affect how we spend and invest our money, and determine the types of public policies that make sense. Even if it is not possible to develop a perfect forecast of future food prices, it is helpful to identify some warning signs that prices are likely to rise or fall.

Given the size and complexity of the world food system, the list of forces that determine the price of food is incredibly long. This book is not intended to examine every aspect of the issue, but instead focuses on a few of the most important factors:

- Biofuel production
- Energy prices
- Government policies
- The weather
- Economic growth and changing diets
- The value of the U.S. dollar
- Speculation

None of the items on the list would surprise anyone who has been following news reports about food prices. Indeed, a lot of the reporting did get important parts of the story right. Expanding biofuel production *has* increased the demand for grain and vegetable oil with impacts across the entire food system. Higher energy prices *do* increase the price of producing, processing, and transporting food and encourage the growth of the biofuel industry. Government policies *did* contribute to the increase in world food prices by supporting growth in biofuel production, restricting food exports, and eliminating buffer stock programs. Poor weather in 2006 and 2007 *did* reduce grain production in a number of key exporting countries. Economic growth in China and elsewhere *has* led to changing diets that have increased the demand for meat and dairy products, with important implications for world trade and food prices. A weaker U.S. dollar *does* contribute to an increase in U.S. food exports and in dollar-denominated prices. Market speculators *can* amplify price swings, and many nontraditional investors were heavily invested in futures markets for farm products.

While many of the conventional explanations for the rise in food prices in 2007 and early 2008 are at least partially correct, the story is often much more complicated. For example, it is true that poor weather reduced grain yields in 2007 in Australia and Europe, but production elsewhere rose and global grain production actually increased. Rising incomes in middle income countries do result in dietary changes that affect world food markets, but these changes didn't suddenly begin in 2006. Changes in currency values mean that price movements do not look the same when expressed in dollars, euro or yen, but food prices increased sharply in every major currency between 2005 and the summer of 2008. Much of the reporting would have led one to believe that food prices could only increase, yet prices for major staple foods declined sharply in the final months of 2008.

The story of biofuels and food prices is anything but simple. The biofuel industry did not fall unexpectedly from the sky, but grew rapidly in response to government policies and energy market developments. In the United States, current policies include minimum use requirements, tariffs on imports and tax benefits for those who blend biofuels with gasoline and diesel fuel. This creates a very complicated relationship between fuel and food markets. Under some circumstances even modest changes in petroleum prices may translate into significant changes in food prices; in other cases the relationship may be weak.

An important argument of this book is that almost all of the major factors that caused food prices to rise from 2005 until the first part of 2008 were reversed and contributed to the decline in food product prices in the final months of 2008. Better weather led to sharply higher yields in Europe and Australia. The world financial crisis reduced purchasing power of countries and individuals, and this translated into lower consumer spending on some types of food. The dollar strengthened, petroleum prices fell, biofuel production growth slowed, policies were reversed, and many speculators abandoned food product markets. Food prices will continue to be volatile as long as the weather varies, the macroeconomy experiences periods of growth and recession, petroleum prices rise and fall, and politicians can change the rules of the game.

This book is an outgrowth of work done by the Food and Agricultural Policy Research Institute (FAPRI), a joint institute of the University of Missouri and Iowa State University. Each year, FAPRI prepares a very detailed set of baseline projections for U.S. and world agricultural markets. These baseline projections are then used as the point of departure for analyses of alternative policies and market conditions. For example, during recent debates on 2007 energy legislation and the 2008 farm bill, FAPRI estimated how food markets would be affected by some of the many policy changes that were proposed.

One thing FAPRI has learned over the years is that people who make and use market projections need a good sense of perspective—and humor. In a rapidly changing world, even the best projections have a very short shelf life. The economic models used to develop the projections necessarily rely on a long series of assumptions, and at least some of these assumptions always prove to be incorrect when viewed with 20-20 hindsight. Just to take three obvious examples, FAPRI baseline projections assume average weather conditions prevail around the world, current policies remain in place, and petroleum prices follow a particular path over time. In reality, the weather is never average, policies change, and petroleum prices evolve differently than anyone could predict. The "garbage-in, garbage-out" rule applies: If the assumptions underlying the baseline are incorrect, the projections will also be incorrect.

For all these reasons, this book uses market projections by FAPRI and other institutions simply to illustrate important points, rather than to predict what will actually happen. If there is one lesson readers should take away from this book, it is that analysts who say they know exactly how food prices will evolve in the future are misleading their audience or fooling themselves. By focusing instead on the factors that will drive future food price changes, the goal is to provide the tools needed to understand a fast-changing world.

Chapters 1 through 8 explain some of the factors that have contributed to recent volatility in food prices. Each chapter starts with a rule of thumb, discusses how it applies to the 2005–2009 period, and then explains how the full story can often be a little more complicated. Chapter 9 takes a longer view, identifying some of the forces that will determine what the price of food will be 10, 20, or 50 years from now. An appendix provides a primer on world food markets as background for the material presented in the rest of the book.

Chapter 1

Biofuel Boom

The mere mention of biofuels can provoke strong responses from people on both sides of the debate. Supporters see biofuels as a great way to reduce reliance on imported petroleum and to promote rural development. Some opponents claim biofuel production is a "crime against humanity" that takes food from the poor.[1]

Biofuel opponents call this the "food versus fuel" debate and argue that the world's corn, sugar, and vegetable oil should be used to feed people rather than fuel vehicles. Biofuel supporters argue that the world's farmers are perfectly capable of producing both food and fuel. The two sides argue about the environmental benefits and costs of biofuels and about the net effect of biofuels on the world's use of fossil fuels. They also argue about the impacts of biofuel production on food prices.

When food prices were rising sharply in 2007 and early 2008, many opponents of biofuels pointed at the rapid increase in biofuel production as the principal culprit. Biofuel supporters argued that rising food prices were due to a wide range of other factors, and that increased biofuel production played at most a minor role. A parlor game developed of estimating how much of the increase in food prices could be attributed to biofuel production. Players could not agree on the rules of the game and the result was widely differing estimates that simply added to the confusion.

Biofuel supporters and opponents have both overstated their cases. Biofuels played an important role in the rise and fall of food prices between 2005 and 2009, but other forces were also at play.

Anything that affects the amount of food produced or consumed in the world will have some impact on food prices. When drought reduces Australian wheat production, it raises the price of food. When increasing incomes cause more meat consumption in China, it raises the price of food. When more of the world's corn, sugar, and vegetable oil is used to produce fuel instead of food, it raises the price of food. Thus, a first rule of thumb: *Increasing biofuel production raises the price of food.*

Rules of thumb are helpful guides, as long as one understands their limitations. Biofuel production is just one of many factors affecting food prices. If increases in food production are rapid enough, food prices may fall even if biofuel production is increasing. If higher incomes cause food consumption to increase, food prices may rise even if biofuel production is declining. Increases in biofuel production, however, will make food prices higher than they would have been without the new source of demand.

The 2005-2009 Experience

The growth in biofuel production between 2005 and the middle of 2008 was nothing short of amazing. In the United States, for example, ethanol production more than doubled in less than three years (Figure 1.1). A rapidly increasing share of the U.S. corn crop was devoted to ethanol production, and this limited the amount of grain available to provide food to people and feed to livestock around the world. At the same time, Brazil was rapidly increasing its production of ethanol from sugar. The European Union was increasing its production of biodiesel from rapeseed oil, and biodiesel production from other vegetable oils was rising rapidly in the United States and other countries.

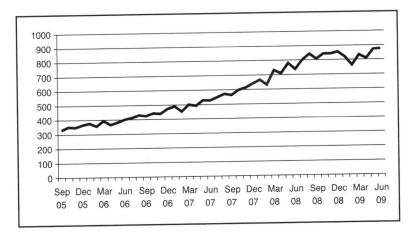

Figure 1.1 *U.S. monthly fuel ethanol production, million gallons*

Source: Author calculations based on data from the U.S. Energy Information Administration, September 2009.

Food prices also increased sharply between 2005 and the middle of 2008. FAO's index of world food prices rose 85 percent between September 2005 and its peak in June 2008 (Figure 1.2). The simultaneous increase in ethanol production and food prices led many to conclude that increased ethanol production was the cause of higher food prices.

When the price of tortillas rose in Mexico, people blamed the expansion of ethanol production in the United States. When vegetable oil prices rose around the world, people blamed the expansion of biodiesel production. The fundamental point of biofuel critics is valid: When corn, sugar, and vegetable oils are used to make biofuels, the immediate and direct effect is to reduce food availability, and the result is higher food prices. While the direction of the effect is clear, the size of the effect is not.

11

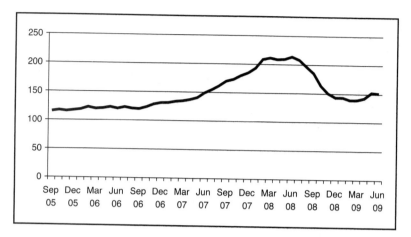

Figure 1.2   *FAO world food price index*

Source: Food and Agriculture Organization of the United Nations, September 2009.

The critical question, then, is just how important the increase in biofuel production was in the context of all the other factors that were pushing up food prices between 2005 and the middle of 2008. The question remains controversial, not just because powerful interests on all sides of the debate cannot afford to cede the argument, but because the facts themselves are complex and open to alternative explanations.

Start with the simple question: How large was the impact of increased ethanol production on world cereal markets between 2005 and 2008? To examine that question, consider what happened to world cereal consumption between the 2005/2006 and 2007/2008 marketing years (Table 1.1).[2] Depending on how one chooses to tell the story, the role of ethanol can appear relatively small or absolutely critical.

Table 1.1   *Cereal Consumption, Million Metric Tons*

World Consumption	2005/2006	2007/2008	Absolute Change	Percentage Change
Corn	705	770	66	9.3%
Wheat	617	612	-5	-0.8%
Milled rice	413	426	14	3.3%
Other cereals	286	285	-1	-0.2%
All cereals	2,020	2,094	74	3.7%
Corn used in U.S. ethanol plants	41	77	37	90.2%
World cereal use except corn used in U.S. ethanol plants	1,979	2,016	37	1.9%
Corn used in U.S. ethanol plants as share of world cereal use	2.0%	3.7%		

Source: Author calculations based on USDA PSD Online data set and World Agricultural Supply and Demand Estimates, September 2009.

The Story as Told by a Biofuel Supporter

In 2007/2008, the world used about 2.1 billion metric tons of cereals (corn, wheat, rice, barley, sorghum, oats, millet, rye, and mixed grains). The vast majority of that was used to feed the people, livestock, and poultry of the world. The amount of corn used by ethanol plants in the United States was only 77 million metric tons, or less than 4 percent of total world cereal use. Even that overestimates the amount of grain diverted from food and feed markets, as ethanol plants produce both ethanol and a variety of other products, including livestock feed and vegetable oil. Correcting for these other feeds and foods produced by ethanol plants, the actual amount of U.S. corn that was turned into ethanol in 2007/2008 was less than 3 percent of the world's cereal consumption.

If ethanol use of corn was such a modest share of world cereal use, it does not make sense to blame ethanol for the rise in food prices. If the growth in ethanol production was the main factor behind rising cereal prices, you would have expected to see an absolute reduction in the availability of cereals for food and feed. Table 1.1 shows, however, that the total use of cereals for food and feed increased by 37 million metric tons between 2005/2006 and 2007/2008. The world demonstrated that it can produce both food and fuel, and critics need to look elsewhere to explain the rise in food prices.

For example, note the drop in wheat consumption, easily explained by poor wheat yields in major exporting countries in 2006 and 2007. Also note that corn consumption grew far more than the increase in ethanol use, showing that farmers could and did expand corn production, and demonstrating that world corn demand was increasing for reasons beyond the increase in ethanol consumption. Maybe growth in ethanol production was part of the story of rising food prices, but the figures clearly demonstrate that other factors were also in play.

The Story as Told by a Biofuel Critic

The data in Table 1.1 confirm that ethanol was a critical factor behind the rise in cereal prices in particular and food prices in general. Between 2005/2006 and 2007/2008, world cereal consumption increased by 74 million metric tons. Over those same two years, U.S. ethanol plants increased their use of corn by 37 million metric tons.

In other words, the increase in the use of corn by U.S. ethanol plants accounted for half of the total increase in cereal use by the entire world. The increase in other, non-ethanol-related uses of cereals was only about 2 percent—less than the increase in the world's population. In other words, U.S. ethanol plants accounted for the entire increase in world per-capita grain consumption between 2005/2006 and 2007/2008.

It does not matter that ethanol still accounts for a fairly modest share of global cereal use. What matters is that the share increased very sharply in a very short period of time. Annual changes in world cereal consumption are usually relatively small. The world's population grows at a predictable rate, and factors such as changes in income rarely cause very large annual changes in world per-capita grain consumption. In the past, it might have been possible to deal with such a sudden change in consumption by drawing down global cereal stocks. However, world cereal stocks are now much lower relative to consumption than they were even a decade ago, so further reducing stocks is not a viable option.

In other words, the rapid increase in ethanol use of cereals disrupted the delicate balance between supply and demand in world cereal markets. The result was a dramatic increase in cereal prices in particular and food prices in general.

So Who's Right?

Both sides of the debate can tell their stories by providing the appropriate spin on the data reported in Table 1.1. Both versions of the story make defensible points, but both also overlook inconvenient facts and arguments. Ethanol remains a relatively small share of world cereal production, for example, but ethanol production also accounted for a large share of the increase in world cereal consumption in precisely the years when cereal prices were rising. Likewise, it is true that growth in ethanol consumption disrupted the supply-demand balance in world cereal markets, but so did all the other factors discussed in this book.

In the final months of 2008, prices for cereals, vegetable oils, and other food products retreated from their peak levels. Developments in biofuel production are again a part of the story, and once again the story can be told in different ways by biofuel supporters and opponents. As shown in Figure 1.1, the growth in U.S. ethanol production essentially ground to a halt from August 2008 through April 2009. U.S. biodiesel production declined and biofuel production growth in other countries also slowed or even reversed.

Biofuel proponents correctly point out that U.S. ethanol production did not significantly decline, but merely leveled off in the final months of 2008, yet world cereal prices fell sharply. This supports their argument that changes in food prices are largely due to factors unrelated to biofuel production. On the other hand, biofuel opponents can correctly point out that the slowdown in biofuel production growth was itself an important change in market trends. It should not be surprising that cereal prices fell from their peak levels given slower growth in biofuel production, but it should also not be surprising that cereal prices remained well above the levels that prevailed in previous years.

It would be a mistake to claim there is any sort of consensus about the role of biofuels in food price developments between 2005 and 2009. Distilling all the arguments, however, it is possible to draw some broad conclusions. The rapid increase in biofuel production between 2005 and the middle of 2008 increased the total world demand for grain, sugar and vegetable oil. This increase in demand helped shift the balance in world food markets, putting significant upward pressure on food prices. The slowdown in biofuel industry growth in the final months of 2008 likewise was an important factor behind a decline in prices for many food products. However, other factors were also clearly at play; biofuels were just one part of the story.

Why the Story Is a Little More Complicated

Nothing about biofuels is simple, so it should not be surprising that the full story of biofuels and food prices is even more complicated than described so far. The growth of the biofuel industry has had wide-ranging impacts on food markets in recent years, and it set in motion a series of events that will be playing out for years to come.

Getting from Biofuel Production to Mexican Tortilla Prices

When an increase in ethanol production increases the demand for corn in the United States, it is easy to understand why this results in higher corn prices in U.S. markets. It may be less obvious why this should necessarily result in higher prices for other food products in other countries. In some cases, the connections are direct, clear, strong, and immediate; in other cases the connections are indirect, murky, weak, and deferred.

If you accept that increased ethanol production causes higher U.S. corn prices, it makes sense that the price of foods made from U.S. corn should also increase. However, the value of the corn used to make a bag of corn chips or a box of breakfast cereal is just a few cents. Likewise, the cost of the high-fructose corn syrup in a typical soft drink is a very small proportion of the retail price. Even doubling the price of corn will only have a modest direct impact on the prices for many consumer foods.

Now consider a case that remains controversial—the impact of increased U.S. ethanol production on tortilla prices in Mexico. The connection may appear simple and direct. Under terms of the North American Free Trade Agreement (NAFTA), Mexico no longer imposes any tariffs or other restrictions on imports of corn from the United States. Higher prices for corn in the U.S. market mean higher prices for U.S. corn imported by Mexico. Those higher corn prices should translate into higher prices for tortillas and all other products made from corn.

The story is not quite that simple. The United States primarily produces and exports yellow corn. In Mexico, yellow corn is used almost exclusively as feed for livestock and poultry. Tortillas are made primarily from white corn, and almost all of the white corn used to make Mexican tortillas is produced in Mexico. To the extent that these are two distinct products used for two distinct purposes, an increase in the U.S. price of yellow corn does not have a direct and immediate effect on the Mexican price of white corn used to make tortillas. Yet, wholesale prices of white corn in Mexico City increased by 66 percent between 2005 and 2008.[3]

Some would argue that the rise in Mexican white corn prices was just a coincidence, and that many factors other than growth in the U.S. ethanol industry were the cause. Still, it is not all that difficult to make a connection between U.S. ethanol production and white corn prices in Mexico. When the price of imported yellow corn rose, Mexican livestock producers experienced a large increase in feed prices. Normally, white corn sells for more than yellow corn, so livestock producers would have no incentive to feed it to livestock.

The large increase in yellow corn prices meant there were some places in Mexico where white corn was cheaper than yellow corn. At least a few livestock feeders started feeding white corn to livestock, and this meant less white corn was available for the domestic food market, leading to higher prices. The sharp increase in yellow corn prices may have caused at least some Mexican farmers who would normally plant white corn to plant yellow corn instead. These shifts in corn consumption and production did not have to be very large to have an important impact on Mexican white corn prices. Corn accounts for a large portion of the cost of making tortillas in Mexico, so higher white corn prices translate directly into significantly higher prices for tortillas.

Getting from Biofuel Production to Wheat, Rice, and Soybean Prices

In the United States, almost all ethanol was made from corn between 2005 and 2009. Although some plants in Europe and elsewhere made ethanol from wheat and other cereals, ethanol accounted for only a tiny share of world use of cereals other than corn. Just as in the case of Mexican white corn, however, ethanol production can have an effect on wheat and rice prices even if most ethanol is made from corn.

When corn prices increase, at least a few consumers will buy fewer products made from corn and more products made from other cereals. This effect is typically not very large, especially among higher-income consumers. For example, it is not likely that many U.S. consumers would buy fewer corn chips and more pretzels made from wheat just because the cost of a bag of corn chips increases by a couple of cents. On the other hand, low-income consumers might eat fewer tortillas and instead eat more rice or bread when corn prices increase. By encouraging increased consumption of other grains, higher corn prices cause at least some increase in wheat and rice prices as well.

Livestock producers are even more sensitive to an increase in the price of corn relative to the price of other competing feeds. If corn prices increase, the response will be to feed less corn and more sorghum, wheat, and other feeds. This increase in use for competing cereals causes their prices to increase until they are no longer such a bargain relative to corn.

Finally, farmers trying to decide which crop to plant usually want to grow the crop that makes them the most money. If corn prices are expected to increase, farmers will plant more acres of corn and fewer acres of competing crops. In the United States, this happened most dramatically in 2007 (Figure 1.3). In part because people knew that ethanol production was likely to rise in 2007 and 2008, corn purchasers were willing to offer a high price for corn planted in 2007. This caused many farmers to shift at least part of their cropland to corn and away from soybeans and other competing crops. The result was the largest U.S. corn acreage since World War II. This helped keep corn prices from rising even higher in 2007 and early 2008, but it also meant that production of soybeans and other crops was reduced. Lower soybean production, in turn, contributed to sharply higher prices for the soybean crop harvested in late 2007.

These acreage shifts have implications for crop prices for years to come. In 2008, U.S. soybean acreage recovered and corn acreage retreated somewhat. This happened even as corn prices reached record highs in the spring and summer of 2008. Why did farmers not increase their corn acreage even further in 2008 in response to strong corn prices? One reason was that the sharp increase in corn acreage in 2007 disrupted normal crop rotations. Many farmers plant corn in a field one year and soybeans in the same field the following year. This has a number of agronomic advantages, so farmers are reluctant to deviate from this normal crop rotation. The large increase in corn acreage in 2007 was only possible because many farmers planted corn in the same fields where they had planted corn in the previous year.

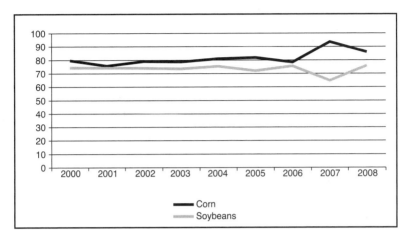

Figure 1.3 *U.S. corn and soybean area planted, million acres*

Source: USDA's National Agricultural Statistics Service, June 2009.

One hectare equals 2.47 acres.

Many of these farmers were eager to get back to more normal crop rotations, so they had an incentive to plant more soybeans and less corn in 2008. Higher soybean prices also encouraged farmers to expand soybean production at the expense of corn in 2008.

Rising input costs also played a role in 2008 crop production choices. Farmers around the world wanted to take advantage of high crop prices, resulting in strong demand for fertilizer to increase crop yields. This increase in demand for fertilizer and increasing energy prices resulted in higher fertilizer prices. Corn production is more dependent on fertilizer than is soybean production, so higher fertilizer prices had the effect of discouraging corn production and encouraging soybean production. For all these reasons, U.S. farmers shifted some land from corn back into soybean production in 2008.

This reduction in U.S. corn acreage, combined with fears that unfavorable weather might reduce 2008 corn yields, made many people worry that there would not be enough corn produced in 2008 to satisfy the demand from the ethanol sector and all the other users of U.S. corn. This contributed to record-high corn prices in mid-2008. Prices fell when it became clear that 2008 crop yields in the United States and other countries would be better than previously expected, and when a wide range of factors, including a slowdown in ethanol production growth, resulted in less grain demand than anticipated.

Soybean prices are also tied to biofuel production in another way. Rapid increases in production of biodiesel in the United States, Europe, and other countries contributed to a sharp increase in the demand for the vegetable oils and animal fats used to produce biodiesel. When the price of one vegetable oil goes up, at least some consumers will try to shift to other, cheaper oils. The ultimate consequence is that the prices for all vegetable oils tend to increase whenever the demand for one type of oil rises. When soybean oil prices increase, processors can afford to pay more for raw soybeans, and the result is higher prices for soybeans.

In the final months of 2008, biodiesel production in the United States declined, and a variety of other factors also contributed to lower prices for vegetable oils. Because soybean crushers earned less from soybean oil sales, soybean prices fell. Most of the value in a bushel of soybeans normally comes from the protein meal, not from the vegetable oil, so biodiesel demand is only part of the story behind the demand for soybeans. However, even protein meal prices are affected indirectly by biofuels, through the effects on soybean production, the prices of competing feeds, and the long-term effects on livestock and poultry production.

Getting from Biofuel Production to Meat, Poultry, and Milk Prices

Most of the world's corn is fed to livestock and poultry. When increased ethanol production results in higher corn prices, the cost of producing beef, pork, chicken, turkey, eggs, and milk also increases. This reduces industry profits and causes at least some producers to scale back production. Lower production, in turn, results in higher prices. In other words, an increase in ethanol production eventually results in higher prices for meat, poultry and milk.

It does not take very long to adjust chicken production, because it only takes a few weeks from the time an egg is hatched to the time a boneless chicken breast shows up in the grocery store. Poultry firms can and do adjust production schedules as circumstances dictate, so when feed prices rise, retail prices for chicken and eggs tend to increase fairly quickly. Because of some basic biology, however, it takes longer for beef, pork, and milk producers to adjust production. For example it takes about two years from the time a calf is born until it becomes a cow ready to bear its own calf. Thus it literally can take years for beef and milk producers to fully adjust to a change in feed prices. Beef, pork, and milk prices will eventually increase when corn prices increase, but the full effects may not be felt for some time.

The effects of biofuel production on animal agriculture are further complicated by the nature of the biofuel production process. Dry mill ethanol plants produce not just ethanol, but also distillers grains, a livestock feed. These distillers grains are fed primarily to cattle, although they can also be fed to hogs and poultry in limited amounts. When ethanol production from corn increases, distillers grains production also increases, and this replaces at least some of the corn removed from the market by ethanol plants. However, most of the calories in corn are turned into ethanol, so the net effect of an increase in ethanol production is to reduce total feed availability.

Biodiesel production from soybean oil also has complex effects on the feed and animal sectors. By increasing the demand for soybean oil and soybeans, biodiesel production results in higher soybean prices. Higher soybean prices cause increased production of soybeans and soybean meal. More soybean meal production translates into lower soybean meal prices, which actually reduces livestock feed costs. However, the full effects of increased biodiesel production on feed prices are not so clear. That is because higher soybean prices also result in less production of corn, and that means higher corn prices. The net effect of increased biodiesel production, therefore, may be to raise the cost of feed to livestock that primarily consume corn and other grains, even if it might reduce the cost of feed for poultry that consume a lot of soybean meal.

When ethanol production from corn increases, feed prices increase. Higher feed prices eventually mean less livestock and poultry production, and this means higher prices for meat, poultry, and milk. Biodiesel from vegetable oil may not have the same effects on meat production and prices, but by driving up the price of vegetable oil, it increases the price of salad dressings, cooking oils, and a wide range of processed foods.

Getting from Biofuel Production to Consumer Food Prices

If biofuel production increases the prices of a wide range of products sold by farmers, it would seem obvious that the result would be an increase in consumer food prices. However, there are a lot of steps between the farm and the consumer. Food products have to be processed, packaged, and delivered to supermarkets and restaurants. Each step along the way incurs additional costs, and may obscure or amplify price changes occurring at the farm level.

In high-income countries like the United States, only a modest fraction of the consumer food dollar goes to farmers. As described in greater detail in the appendix, only about 19 percent of U.S. consumer food spending goes to pay farmers for the food they produce. The rest is split among all the other parts of the food supply chain, from trucking firms to food processors to advertisers to food retailers.

Post-farm labor costs, for example, account for twice as much of the consumer food dollar as the price paid to farmers for the food they produce.[4]

Because there are so many steps between the farm and the consumer, prices usually change proportionally less at the consumer level than they do at the farm level. Even though prices for some food products doubled at the farm level between 2005 and 2008, the increase in U.S. consumer food prices was only 4.0 percent in 2007 and 5.5 percent in 2008. In fact, some of that increase in consumer food prices cannot be attributed to changes in farm-level prices, but rather to higher energy prices that increased the cost of transporting and processing food. U.S. consumer food price inflation slowed in the final months of 2008, and actually was slightly negative in the first few months of 2009.[5]

In lower-income countries, consumers tend to eat more staple foods, and less value is added to food after it leaves the farm. As a result, the sharp increase in world cereal prices from 2005 to 2008 translated into larger increases in consumer food prices in low-income countries than in the United States. For example, FAO reported that consumer food prices in developing countries rose by an average of 13.5 percent in the year ending in February 2008.[6]

Cherry Picking

Just as biofuel supporters and opponents pick the facts that bolster their arguments, the discussion here has been selective in the evidence used to tell the story of how biofuel production affects food prices. Inconvenient facts can sometimes mess up a perfectly good story.

For example, consider the simple question of how much U.S. corn has been used by U.S. ethanol plants and how this has affected other uses of corn. It is true that there was a large increase in the amount of corn used in ethanol production between 2005/2006 and 2007/2008. Some have argued that this large increase in ethanol use of corn squeezed out other uses and pushed up corn prices. Yet the data show that U.S. corn exports increased substantially in 2007/2008 (Figure 1.4). How could the United States sharply increase both its ethanol use of corn and its corn exports in the same year? Biofuel supporters say this refutes the premise of those citing a conflict between food and fuel; the evidence shows that we can produce both food and fuel.

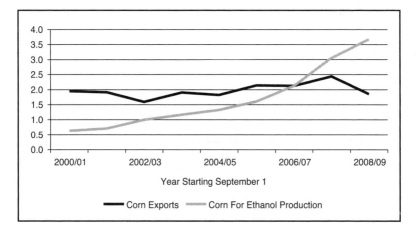

Figure 1.4 *U.S. corn exports and corn used for ethanol production, billion bushels*

Source: USDA's World Agricultural Supply and Demand Estimates, September 2009.

One metric ton equals 39.4 bushels of corn.

What the simultaneous increase in U.S. corn exports and corn used for ethanol production shows is that the story is far from simple. If ethanol production were the only cause of rising corn prices, one would not have expected exports to also increase in 2007/2008. Normally, one would expect higher corn prices to reduce U.S. corn exports, as producers in other countries increase production to benefit from high corn prices and users of corn in other countries try to find alternatives to expensive U.S. corn. However, U.S. corn exports increased in 2007/2008 for all of the reasons described in later chapters—reduced grain production in Europe, strong economic growth around the world, a weak dollar, and more. The United States was able to increase both ethanol use and exports at the same time without running out of corn because U.S. farmers planted more corn and harvested a record crop. That increase in corn production would not have happened, however, had it not been for the anticipated increase in corn prices. If anything, it is evidence that it is possible to satisfy rapidly growing demand for both food and fuel, but at the cost of higher food prices.

Now consider estimates of U.S. corn exports and corn used for ethanol production in the 2008/2009 marketing year (the final data points in Figure 1.4). Even though ethanol production growth essentially stopped in August 2008, the total amount of corn used for ethanol production between September 2008 and August 2009 was expected to far exceed ethanol use of corn during the previous marketing year. This does not seem to fit very well with the story that a slowdown in ethanol production contributed to the large decline in corn prices in the final months of 2008. On the other hand, the decline in corn exports in 2008/2009 suggests that weakness in demand from the rest of the world for U.S. corn was a cause of lower corn prices. That weakness resulted from the recovery of grain production in other countries, the slowdown in the world economy, the strengthening of the dollar, and all the factors described in later chapters.

This brings up another inconvenient fact. It is true that prices for corn and many other food products peaked in mid 2008 and fell sharply in the final months of the year. However, it turns out that the average price U.S. farmers received for the crop they harvested in the final months of 2008 was about the same as the price they received for the crop harvested a year earlier.[7] In 2007/2008, prices rose to reach record highs near the end of the year. In 2008/2009, prices started very high and then fell, but the annual average was about the same. The same story is true for wheat and soybeans, too. Farmers do not sell all of their grain immediately after harvest; many spread their sales out over months or even years. One reason 2008/2009 average prices paid to farmers remained high is that many farmers took advantage of high prices and used forward contracts and futures markets to sell a portion of their 2008 crop even before that crop was harvested.

Prices for corn, wheat, soybeans, and many other food products declined from their peak values in the final months of 2008, but they remained high by historical standards. One reason prices remained relatively high was that ethanol production remained near the peak level of mid-2008. Normally, one would have expected prices to be much lower in response to record world grain production, a very weak global economy, and a stronger dollar.

Great Expectations

Growth in U.S. ethanol production was very rapid from 2005 until the middle of 2008, but that should hardly have been a surprise to people and firms that bought and sold grain in world markets. To the extent everyone knew that ethanol production was likely to increase, grain traders should have built that knowledge into their bids and offers even before the actual increases in ethanol production occurred.

As evidence that the increase in ethanol production should not have been a surprise, consider publicly available information about the number of ethanol plants operating and under construction on different dates (Table 1.2). During the height of the ethanol boom in September 2007, U.S. plants that could produce 6.9 billion gallons of ethanol in a year were in operation. In response to large actual and expected profits, an incredible 6.8 billion gallons of additional produc-

Table 1.2   *U.S. Ethanol Plant Capacity*

	September2007	September2008	June2009
	(billion gallons per year)		
Operating capacity	6.9	10.4	10.8
Capacity under construction	6.8	3.4	1.9
Idle capacity	NA*	NA*	1.8
Sum	13.7	13.8	14.5

Source: Renewable Fuels Association website, accessed September 28, 2007, September 25, 2008, and June 9, 2009.

*Idle capacity was not reported in 2007 or 2008.

tion capacity was under construction. This was widely available information, and was a major factor contributing to higher corn prices in 2007.

Most people were reasonably certain that those plants under construction would be completed and that they would operate, and it was easy to calculate approximately how much corn they would need. For example, as early as May 2007, the U.S. Department of Agriculture estimated that U.S. ethanol plants would use 3.40 billion bushels of corn during the 2007/2008 marketing year.[8] Final estimates for the 2007/2008 marketing year indicate that actual corn use by ethanol plants was about 3.05 billion bushels. In other words, as early as May 2007, corn market participants had information that ethanol use of corn would increase sharply in 2007/2008, and if there were any surprises, it was that actual ethanol use was lower than originally expected.

This raises an important question. If "everybody knew" that ethanol use would increase at least as rapidly as it did, why did corn prices continue to increase after May 2007? Recall that corn prices did not peak until June 2008, at levels far above those of a year earlier. For example, the U.S. export price of corn increased by 79 percent between May 2007 and June 2008.[9] If the increase in ethanol use was fully anticipated by traders in the corn market, prices should not have increased so much after May 2007 unless other unexpected factors were also affecting the supply and demand for corn.

The data in Table 1.2 show that the surprise was not rapid new investment in ethanol plants. By September 2008, a lot of new ethanol plants had been completed, but almost no new plants had started construction relative to the previous year. Operating capacity increased by about 3.5 billion gallons between September 2007 and September 2008, but the amount of capacity under construction fell by 3.4 billion gallons. The implied 100 million gallon increase in the total amount of ethanol capacity built or under construction is hardly enough to explain a large increase in corn prices.

Finally, note the final column of Table 1.2, By June 2009, more ethanol plants had been completed, so the amount of capacity under construction fell to just 1.9 billion gallons. However, the actual operating capacity had increased only slightly since September 2008, as a number of ethanol plants were sitting idle.[10] The profitability of ethanol production plummeted in 2008, and this strongly discouraged new investment in the industry and even resulted in idle plant capacity.

None of this suggests that increased ethanol production was not a major factor behind rising prices for corn in particular and food in general. However, it does make clear that other factors were in play as well. Massive investment in ethanol capacity and growth in ethanol production clearly pushed up corn prices in 2006 and 2007, but other forces were responsible for much of the increase in corn prices in late 2007 and early 2008.

Back to the Parlor Game

Arguments about precisely how much of the increase in food prices between 2005 and 2008 was caused by biofuel production are not going to be resolved easily. Estimates by analysts are all across the board, and are difficult to compare. Some of the larger estimates are obtained by focusing on cereal markets and by being inclusive in deciding what effects are properly attributed to biofuel production. Smaller estimates are obtained by looking at a broader range of foods but defining the effects that can be attributed to biofuel production more narrowly. Economists argue about whose model is better for analyzing this and other questions, but usually the biggest differences in results are not because of the models used but because of the assumptions made.

Instead of thoroughly reviewing all the competing studies to try to prove who is right and who is wrong, consider a simple math problem. Suppose a small car dealership increased its sales this year by ten cars. The dealership has three salespeople. John sold ten more cars this year, and so did Jane, but Frank sold ten fewer cars this year. So suppose the question is posed, how much of the dealership's increase in car sales can be attributed to John? If you take John's ten additional cars sold and divide it by the ten-car increase in total car sales by the dealership, you could conclude that John accounted for 100 percent of the increase in dealership sales. Likewise, you could do the same math and conclude that Jane also accounted for 100 percent of the increase in dealership sales. Both estimates are mathematically correct, but it does not seem very helpful to conclude that two salespeople each accounted for the entire increase in dealership sales.

The same sort of problem occurs when you ask how much of the increase in food prices is due to any one factor. In any year, some factors are pushing up food prices and other factors are pushing down food prices. Food prices increased so much between 2005 and the middle of 2008 precisely because so many forces were all pushing prices up at the same time, and food prices fell in the final months of 2008 because so many forces were pushing prices down at the same time. However, even over the 2005 through 2008 period, there were some countervailing factors. For example, while unfavorable weather in some key countries pushed up food prices in 2007, other countries had good growing conditions in 2007 and even harvested record crops.

The point of this discussion is to reinforce the simple point that you need to be cautious in interpreting statistics and carefully ask the right questions. In any debate, extreme partisans will use and abuse statistics to make their points. Even the most fair-minded analyst will use statistics to tell a story, perhaps without even recognizing that only part of the story is being told. In the debate over biofuels and their effects on food prices, it is easy to find examples of misused statistics to support a case and of analysts without an axe to grind who miss important aspects of the story.

Looking Ahead

Biofuel production clearly played a major role in food price developments between 2005 and 2009. As fun as it is to argue about history, though, it is probably more important to understand what role biofuels will play in the future. In 2009, biofuel production still uses only a fairly modest share of the world's grain, oilseeds, and sugar. If that share does not grow over time, biofuel production is likely to fade as a major concern in world food markets. However, if biofuel production grows in the years and decades ahead, it will matter tremendously how biofuels are produced.

Currently, almost all biofuels are made from raw materials that can also be used as human food or livestock feed. If the future of biofuels is the present writ large, the key question will be whether the world can expand production of corn, sugar, and vegetable oil fast enough to satisfy demand for both food and fuel. New technologies are intended to make fuels from other raw materials. If these new technologies become commercially viable, they will have new and different effects on food prices. Just what those will be is very difficult to anticipate without knowing what raw materials will be used.

If biofuels can be made from materials that are currently wasted or on land not used for agricultural production, it may be possible to increase biofuel production without having any important effects on food production and prices. However, there are very few materials that are truly "waste" and very little land that could be used to produce biofuels that does not already have some agricultural use. Crop residues, such as the part of the corn plant left over after the grain is harvested, may be one potential source of raw materials for future biofuel production, but removing those residues has at least some impact on soil fertility that would need to be offset to maintain food production.

Likewise, some have argued that making ethanol from a crop like switchgrass (a tall perennial grass) that cannot be used as a human food would alleviate food versus fuel concerns. However, even switchgrass production would displace some other agricultural use of land in most cases—less land would be planted to food and feed crops, or less land would be used as pasture for livestock. Unless there is an offsetting factor, the result would be at least some reduction in crop or livestock production and an increase in food prices. This is not to suggest that all biofuels are created equal when it comes to food price effects, but only to clarify that even biofuels made from nonfood raw materials can still have impacts on food prices.

The discussion so far has focused on the effects of biofuel production on food prices. No attempt has been made to explain why biofuels are produced in the first place. The next two chapters examine two of the main reasons biofuels are produced and used: energy markets and government policies.

Chapter 2

Tell Me the Oil Price

Food and energy markets have long been intertwined. When oil and natural gas prices increase, farmers face higher prices for fuel and fertilizer, so crop and livestock production costs increase. Higher fuel prices also increase the costs of processing and transporting food to final consumers. These higher costs eventually translate into higher food prices.

The effects of energy prices on food production and transportation costs are hardly new. What has changed is that oil prices now also have a major impact on the demand for farm products because of the growing biofuel industry. High oil prices make biofuel production more profitable, and this encourages the industry to expand. With current technologies, more biofuel production means more grain, sugar, and vegetable oil is used by biofuel plants to make ethanol and biodiesel. The result is higher prices, not just for the farm products used to produce biofuels, but also for food in general.

The reverse is also true. Lower energy prices reduce farm production costs and the cost of getting food from the farm to the plate. Lower oil prices also are likely to make biofuel production less profitable, and this translates into less demand for grain, sugar, and vegetable oil. Just as rising oil prices can push up food prices, falling oil prices can put downward pressure on food prices. This brings us to another rule of thumb: *Food prices tend to move with crude oil prices.*

The linkages between energy and food prices could get even stronger in the years ahead. The experience of 2005–2009 shows that biofuel production can increase very rapidly when it is expected to be profitable and that biofuel industry growth can be halted when it is not. The price of oil is not the only reason biofuel producers make or lose money—factors ranging from government policies to the weather can also be vitally important. Still, the linkages among oil prices, biofuel production, and food prices can be very strong.

Some will take the argument to its logical conclusion and say, "If you tell me the price of oil, I'll tell you the price of food." There are a number of reasons why the linkage between energy and food markets will not be that strong and predictable, especially in the short run. However, it is true that, given current technologies and government policies, the price of oil essentially puts a floor under food prices in the longer run.

If the price of oil is consistently too high relative to the price of corn, for example, ethanol production will be very profitable and people will build more ethanol plants. The resulting increase in the use of corn will raise corn prices until it is no longer profitable to build and operate more ethanol plants. In the long run, the price of corn can neither be so high that ethanol plants all lose money nor so low that ethanol production is hugely profitable. Rising prices for corn eventually translate into higher prices for food in general. New technologies and changes in policy will change the relationship between energy and food prices, but there are likely to be continued strong linkages for years to come.

The 2005–2009 Experience

The swings in crude oil prices were even more exaggerated than the swings in food prices between 2005 and 2009. The price of West Texas Intermediate oil, the U.S. benchmark, rose from $60 per barrel in March 2007 to over $130 per barrel in June and July 2008 before collapsing to around $40 per barrel at the end of 2008 and then recovering to about $70 per barrel in June 2009 (Figure 2.1).

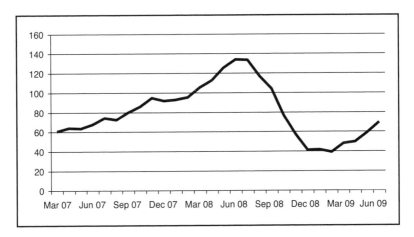

Figure 2.1   *Crude oil prices, dollars per barrel*

Source: West Texas Intermediate oil monthly prices from the U.S. Energy Information Administration, September 2009.

Like the story of the boom and bust in food prices, the story of the boom and bust in oil prices is complex. In fact, two of the factors behind recent changes in food prices also played an important role in the oil market. Rapid economic growth in China, India, and many other countries led to construction booms and more vehicles on the road. As a result, fuel demand grew rapidly, putting upward pressure on oil prices. When the world financial crisis came to a head in the final months of 2008, the sharp slowdown in economic growth dramatically reduced the demand for fuel around the world, driving down oil prices.

Exchange rate movements also affected oil prices, just as they did food prices. Oil prices are quoted in dollars. When the dollar was weakening against most major currencies from 2005 until the middle of 2008, it helped push up the price of oil measured in dollars per barrel, but held down the price measured in other currencies. The strengthening of the dollar in the final months of 2008 had the opposite effect. In the spring and summer of 2009, renewed weakening of the dollar contributed to a rebound in oil prices. Oil price movements were also driven by geopolitical events, the decisions of oil-producing countries and much more.

During the 2005–2009 period, the ties between oil and food markets strengthened considerably. One indicator of these ties is the correlation between oil and corn prices (Figure 2.2). Between March 2007 and June 2008, both oil and corn prices increased dramatically. Oil prices more than doubled, and corn prices increased almost as much. By no means did the two prices march in lockstep. For example, oil prices rose by almost 10 percent in July 2007, but corn prices fell significantly that month, in part because favorable weather improved prospects for a large U.S. corn crop. Still, both prices rose sharply and reached record highs at about the same time.

After hitting their mid-year peaks, the prices of both oil and corn crashed in the final months of 2008. Oil prices fell by 69 percent between June and December 2008. Corn prices fell by 45 percent

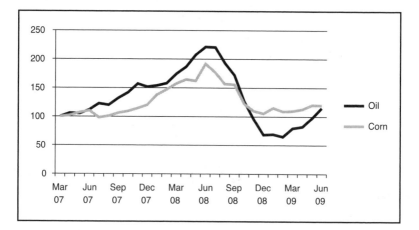

Figure 2.2   *Oil and corn prices, March 2007=100*

Source: Author calculations based on West Texas Intermediate oil prices from the Energy Information Administration and U.S. Gulf corn prices from USDA's Economic Research Service, September 2009.

over the same period. Oil prices rebounded in early 2009, while corn prices were fairly stable. By June 2009, oil and corn prices were both back to levels similar to those prevailing in mid 2007.

Correlation, of course, does not prove causation. Just because oil and corn prices generally moved together in recent years does not prove that one caused the other. It could be a simple matter of coincidence and citation of some selective statistics to tell a story. Alternatively, it is possible that other factors, such as world economic growth and exchange rates, affect both oil prices and food prices in similar ways. That would indicate that oil and food prices share a common set of causes, but they do not necessarily cause each other.

There are good reasons to believe that the correlation between oil and food prices is more than just a coincidence or simply the result of some common underlying causes. Rising oil prices raise the cost of producing, processing, and transporting food and encourage increased production of biofuels. Higher costs and more nonfood demand for agricultural products both result in higher food prices.

Food production costs rose sharply between 2005 and 2008. In the United States, for example, total farm production expenses increased from $220 billion in 2005 to $290 billion in 2008, an increase of 32 percent, and some of the largest increases were in categories directly tied to energy prices.[1] In high-income countries, most of the cost of food is associated with what happens after products leave the farm. Food processing can be energy intensive, and packaging frequently uses petroleum-based raw materials. Transporting food around the world also requires large amounts of oil, of course. The increases in consumer food prices between 2005 and mid 2008 were in part due to rising farm-level prices for wheat, cattle, tomatoes, and other basic farm products. However, rising oil prices also increased the costs of transforming those raw farm products into bread, beef, and salsa and of putting consumer-ready food products on grocery shelves.

The previous chapter detailed the rapid growth in biofuel production between 2005 and the middle of 2008, but did not try to explain *why* biofuel production rose so quickly. Rising oil prices are one important reason. Higher oil prices mean higher prices for gasoline and diesel fuel. When gasoline and diesel fuel prices increase, the prices of ethanol and biodiesel also tend to increase, as fuel sellers and consumers look for alternatives to petroleum-based fuels. Higher biofuel prices make biofuel production more profitable, encouraging investment in new plants and full utilization of existing capacity. To increase biofuel production with current technologies requires that more of the world's grain, sugar, and vegetable oil be converted into fuel, reducing available food supplies and driving up food prices.

When oil prices fell in the final months of 2008, biofuel and food prices fell as well. Lower prices for ethanol and biodiesel discouraged new investment in biofuel plants, slowed construction activity, and even resulted in the idling of biofuel production capacity. The resulting slowdown or outright declines in biofuel production resulted in less demand for raw farm products and made a major contribution to the reduction in food product prices.

Why the Story Is a Little More Complicated

The connections among oil prices, food production costs, biofuel production, and food prices are all very real, but they are also very complicated.

Farm Production Costs and Food Prices

Higher energy prices have direct impacts on farm production costs. Farm tractors and harvesting equipment usually run on diesel fuel. Energy prices affect the cost of irrigating crops, milking cows, and much more. Natural gas is the main raw material used in producing nitrogen fertilizer, and fossil fuels are also used in the production of other agricultural chemicals. Even in countries such as India and China, where levels of mechanization are much lower than in North America or Europe, synthetic fertilizer use levels are quite high.[2] Of course, organic food producers deliberately minimize use of synthetic fertilizers and other agricultural chemicals, and farmers in many low-income countries cannot afford tractors or even fertilizer. Still, most of the world's food production is heavily reliant on fossil fuels.

To get an idea of how important energy prices are to the cost of producing food, consider average budgets for U.S. corn, soybean, and wheat production (Table 2.1). In 2008, U.S. corn farmers spent $43 per acre on fuel purchased to till the soil, plant and harvest the crop, and deliver it to market. Corn producers spent a record $139 per acre on fertilizer in 2008, and the cost of fertilizer was strongly affected by fossil fuel prices. Other cost categories are also affected by energy

Table 2.1 *U.S. Crop Production Expenses, 2008, Dollars per Acre*

	Corn	Soybeans	Wheat
Fertilizer	139.18	25.12	52.51
Fuel	42.64	20.20	25.25
Seed	60.02	44.35	16.02
Other operating costs*	53.85	38.12	31.90
Total operating costs	295.69	127.79	125.68
Land and other overhead	233.69	208.35	151.72
Total costs	529.38	336.13	277.40
Value of production	629.36	446.45	333.83

Source: USDA's Economic Research Service, October 2009.

*Other operating costs include chemicals, machinery repairs, etc., but not the cost of land, machinery depreciation, or other fixed costs.

prices, but generally to a lesser degree. For example, energy prices impact the cost of producing chemicals to kill weeds and insects and of applying those chemicals on farm fields. Even the costs of seed and repairing machinery are affected by energy prices.

Production costs for soybeans and wheat are similar to those for corn in some respects and very different in others. Per-acre costs for both soybeans and wheat are much lower than the per-acre cost of producing corn. In the case of soybeans, the biggest difference is that fertilizer costs are dramatically lower than for corn. This is easily explained, because soybeans have the ability to "fix" nitrogen from the atmosphere (biological nitrogen fixation), whereas corn does not. Thus farmers apply little or no nitrogen fertilizer to soybean fields, but on cornfields they apply large amounts. In the case of wheat, the mix of costs is similar to that for corn, even though the per-acre level of costs is much lower. In the United States, wheat is primarily grown on less productive land and yields are accordingly lower than for corn.[3] Lower yields require less use of fertilizer, and other per-acre costs are also lower. On a per-bushel or per-ton basis, however, U.S. average production costs for wheat are actually higher than for corn.[4]

Fuel and fertilizer expenses are important, but they must be kept in context. For both corn and wheat, fuel and fertilizer accounted for more than 60 percent of operating costs in 2008. However, operating costs do not include the cost of land, machinery replacement, and other overhead costs. Relative to total costs, the fuel and fertilizer share drops below 35 percent. As important as energy prices are in determining crop production costs, a 1 percent increase in energy prices increases total farm production expenses by much less than 1 percent.

In the United States, production of corn, soybeans, and wheat was profitable in 2008 for most farmers. The total farm value of crops produced exceeded total production costs, even after assigning a value to the unpaid labor of farm family members. This has an important implication for the linkage between energy prices and food prices. Suppose prices for oil and natural gas had been slightly higher in 2008. For any given crop price, this would have made crop production less profitable, and it might have caused farmers to shift away from crops that are very energy intensive, like corn, to crops that are less energy intensive, like soybeans. However, as long as most farmers were still able to operate profitably, there is little reason to expect that there would be the sort of large reduction in overall crop production that would result in across-the-board increases in food prices.

In fact, many farmers would not have an incentive to reduce production in the short run even if they were losing money relative to total production costs. So long as the value of crop sales exceeds the level of operating costs, farmers will not have a reason to allow productive cropland to lie idle. In other words, they may lose money growing a crop, but they would lose even more if they choose not to grow a crop—either way, they would still have to pay for land and other fixed expenses. When production costs increase, the result is likely to be downward pressure on farm income and the value of farmland and other farm assets, but there may not be large effects on total crop production and prices.

The experience of 2005–2008 shows higher energy prices do not always translate into lower crop production. Between 2005 and 2008, U.S. farmers actually increased the amount of land they devoted to crop production, as higher crop prices made crop production more profitable in spite of higher fuel and fertilizer costs.[5] Total U.S. fertilizer use also increased slightly between 2005 and 2007, in spite of higher fertilizer prices.[6] Changes in U.S. crop yields between 2005 and 2008 were much more closely tied to changes in the weather than to changes in farm production practices.

It is important not to take this argument too far. Any time farm production costs rise relative to crop prices, at least some farmers will change how they produce crops. While prime farmland in Iowa is unlikely to sit idle, some marginal acres in the Great Plains or in another country may not get planted if production costs rise enough. Over time, farmers will try to find a way to use less fuel and fertilizer when energy prices increase, and this could result in some reduction in crop yields.

The increase in crop prices between 2005 and mid 2008 cannot be explained simply as a matter of farmers passing along higher production costs. Purchasers of corn and soybeans do not care how much it cost to produce a crop; they will only pay the price they have to pay to get the product they desire. Only if higher energy prices cause a reduction in available crop supplies would purchasers pay a higher price. Certainly, rising fuel and fertilizer prices from 2005 until the middle of 2008 affected what crops were planted and how they were produced, but they did not result in the sort of large reductions in total crop production that would fully explain the observed increases in food prices.

Energy prices also affect livestock and poultry production costs. Livestock producers use diesel fuel to operate machinery and electricity to operate fans, milking machines, and other devices. Some cattle producers apply fertilizer to pasture land. Livestock producers are also affected by any change in feed costs that result from changes in energy prices. As with the crop sector, higher production costs only translate into higher prices for meat, poultry, and dairy products if at least some farmers and ranchers reduce production in response to reduced profits.

Fuel Costs and Getting Food from the Farm to the Plate

In high-income countries, most of the consumer's food dollar pays for costs incurred after food leaves the farm, and many of those costs are tied to energy prices. In the United States, for example, farmers receive only about 19 cents of every consumer food dollar, while energy and transportation costs account for about 7.5 cents and packaging another 8 cents.[7] Even if energy prices had no effect on food prices at the farm level, consumer food prices would rise when energy prices increase because of the cost of getting food from the farm to the plate.

Much of the world's food is consumed far from where it is produced. Higher fuel costs have obvious impacts on the cost of moving food across the country or around the world. For example, many of the fresh fruits and vegetables sold in the U.S. Midwest are produced in California, Florida, Mexico, or Chile. U.S. grains and oilseeds are shipped around the world, as are Australian beef, Brazilian orange juice, Colombian coffee, and Spanish olive oil. When fuel prices increase, the cost of delivering food to consumers also increases.

The cost of transportation is one important reason why the price of similar foods can differ significantly by location. Soybean prices in central Illinois are usually quite a bit lower than soybean prices in Europe, for example, simply because of the cost of shipping soybeans down the Mississippi River and across the Atlantic. How large the difference in prices is depends primarily on energy prices and shipping costs. In the 2005/2006 marketing year, for example, soybeans sold for an average of $202 per metric ton in central Illinois, while the import price in the Netherlands was $261, a difference of $59 per metric ton. In part because of the increase in fuel prices, the gap between Illinois and Netherlands soybean prices rose to $98 per metric ton during the 2007/2008 marketing year. Declining oil prices in the final months of 2008 helped bring the price gap back down to $52 per metric ton in the first eight months of the 2008/2009 marketing year.[8] Ocean shipping rates also declined in the last half of 2008 because the global recession reduced world trade and the demand for shipping services.

The per-mile cost of transporting products in large ships is modest relative to the cost of transporting products by truck. This means that food prices can be very different in one part of the country than another. In Mexico, for example, the average price of white corn in the northern state of Sinaloa in 2007 was 2,342 pesos (214 U.S. dollars) per metric ton, while the average price in the southern state of Oaxaca that same year was 3,332 pesos (305 U.S. dollars) per metric ton, a difference of 42 percent.[9] In many African countries with poor road systems, it can cost more to move food a couple of hundred miles from one part of the country to another than it costs to ship food thousands of miles across an ocean.

Energy price increases discourage trade in food among countries and regions. If transportation costs increase enough, regions tend to become more self-sufficient. Many isolated communities around the world are dependent on local food production precisely because it is so difficult and expensive to transport products in and out of remote areas. Still, the size of this effect needs to be kept in perspective. As important as transportation costs are, they constitute a relatively modest share of the cost of most types of food, at least in countries with better-developed transportation systems. Even though petroleum prices more than doubled between March 2007 and June 2008, U.S. consumer food prices only increased by 6.5 percent over the same period.[10]

There are several reasons why many people prefer to buy locally produced foods. Some like to support area farmers and feel that locally produced foods are more likely to be fresh and have a variety of other positive traits. Others deliberately choose to minimize the number of "food miles" traveled by the foods they consume to reduce the use of fossil fuels. Consuming local foods tends to reduce carbon emissions from fossil fuel use, but the general rule does not hold in every case.

For example, a New Zealand study argued that British consumers would actually be responsible for fewer carbon emissions if they consumed lamb and dairy products from New Zealand rather than British lamb and dairy products, in spite of the costs of shipping food halfway around the world. This is possible because New Zealand milk and sheep production is based on year-round pasture grazing, whereas in Britain, cattle and sheep are given supplemental feeds requiring fossil fuels to produce. In comparison, the per-unit and per-mile cost of shipping products on ocean-going vessels is modest.[11]

In spite of all these complications, higher fuel prices do raise transportation costs and discourage trade. Higher transportation costs tend to increase the price of food in importing countries and regions, and reduce the price to exporters.

Energy Prices and the Economics of Biofuel Production

Each country has its own set of policies affecting incentives to produce and consume biofuels. These policies may override market signals. For example, if rules require that each gallon of fuel sold contains fixed percentages of gasoline and ethanol, higher gasoline prices will do nothing to encourage increased ethanol consumption. In the United States, however, the mix of government policies allows fossil fuel prices to have important impacts on the biofuel sector.

The importance to the biofuels sector of both government policies and energy prices is illustrated by looking at the economics of a typical U.S. ethanol plant (Table 2.2). In 2005/2006, ethanol prices were exceptionally high, in part because oil prices had begun their ascent, but mostly because of changes in U.S. policy. Methyl tertiary butyl ether (MTBE) was phased out as a fuel additive because of health concerns, and ethanol was the only practical alternative as an additive to meet regulatory requirements to reduce certain types of air pollution. The resulting increase in ethanol consumption outpaced domestic ethanol production, so ethanol prices were bid up.

Table 2.2   *Ethanol Plant Income and Expenses, Dollars per Gallon*

	2005/2006	2006/2007	2007/2008	2008/2009
Value of ethanol	2.61	2.32	2.40	1.87
Value of distillers grains	0.27	0.34	0.47	0.37
Cost of corn	-0.74	-1.12	-1.54	-1.48
Other operating costs*	-0.58	-0.59	-0.61	-0.58
Net operating return	1.56	0.95	0.71	0.18

Source: Food and Agricultural Policy Research Institute, unpublished estimates, August 2009.

*Other operating costs include fuel, labor, and other operating costs but do not include plant construction expenses and other fixed costs.

High ethanol prices combined with low corn prices made ethanol production very profitable in 2005/2006. The average wholesale price of ethanol in Omaha, Nebraska was about $2.61 per gallon, and a typical ethanol plant could earn an additional $0.27 per gallon by selling distillers grains, a livestock feed co-product of ethanol production. On the cost side of the ledger, low corn prices meant that the corn used to produce a gallon of ethanol only cost about $0.74. Fuel, labor, and other operating costs totaled about $0.58 per gallon, resulting in a net operating return of $1.56 per gallon. The cost of building a new ethanol plant was on the order of $2.00 per gallon of installed capacity, so a single year net return of $1.56 per gallon understandably set off massive investment in new ethanol plants.

Ethanol prices declined in 2006/2007. Increased ethanol production meant there was more than enough ethanol to satisfy the demand for ethanol as a fuel additive replacing MTBE. Corn prices also started to increase, further reducing the profitability of ethanol production. Still, the net operating return for a typical ethanol plant continued to be very large. A plant that started operating on September 1, 2005 could have been fully paid for with the profits made in its first two years of operation.

By 2007/2008, ethanol production had grown to levels where the additive market could only absorb about half of the total production. Ten percent ethanol blends began selling in parts of the country where no regulation required their use and where the nearest ethanol plant was hundreds of miles away. This was possible only when ethanol was priced competitively as a fuel. This meant that the ratio of ethanol to gasoline prices had to decline from the levels that prevailed the previous two years. Luckily for ethanol producers, this change in ethanol pricing occurred precisely when oil and gasoline prices rose to record highs. Ethanol prices increased slightly in 2007/2008, as the effect of higher oil and gasoline prices more than offset the need to reduce the price of ethanol relative to the price of gasoline to encourage expanded ethanol use.

Higher ethanol prices did not translate into larger profits for ethanol producers, however. Sharply higher prices for corn in 2007/2008 outweighed the effect of the slight increase in ethanol prices, so the net operating return to a typical ethanol plant declined. Concerns that profit margins could get even tighter in subsequent years discouraged new industry investment. By the summer of 2008, in spite of record oil prices, many ethanol plants were operating with razor-thin margins because of record-high corn prices.

The collapse in oil and gasoline prices in the final months of 2008 resulted in sharply lower prices for ethanol as well. Although corn prices also fell sharply from their mid-year peak, the marketing year average corn price for 2008/2009 was about the same as the previous year. The result was a tremendous squeeze on ethanol plant profits. The average plant was just able to cover operating costs, which implies that plants with debt and other fixed costs were actually losing money. Some firms even were unable to cover operating costs, so several plants shut down operations.

The high levels of ethanol profitability in 2005/2006 and 2006/2007 could not and did not last. Massive investment resulted in sharp increases in ethanol production, and this increased the demand for corn and contributed to the increase in corn prices. Because of the unanticipated decline in oil prices in the final months of 2008, ethanol profitability dropped to levels that discouraged any new investment. In the long run, ethanol plants should have an average rate of return to investors that is comparable to other businesses. If plants make too much money, more firms will build plants and this will eventually result in lower ethanol prices and higher corn prices. If profitability drops so low that some plants cannot cover operating costs, ethanol production will decline, and this will result in higher ethanol prices and lower corn prices.

This fundamental economic logic means that oil prices, biofuel prices, and food prices are likely to be closely linked in the future. Just as it can take time for changes in corn prices to be fully reflected in prices for other foods, it may also take time for changes in crude oil prices to be fully reflected in the prices of corn, sugar, vegetable oil, and other foods. For example, on any given day, there is only so much existing biofuel production capacity, and once capacity is built, it will be used as long as producers can cover operating costs. Thus, it may take time for changes in oil prices to have their full impact on biofuel production levels. Policies can also weaken or even sever the linkages between oil and food prices. If policies do not get in the way, however, oil prices will eventually have strong effects on biofuel production, and biofuel production will have strong effects on food prices.

Biofuel Effects on Energy Markets

The linkages between energy and food markets do not work in only one direction. When biofuel production increases, there is an effect on the consumption of fossil fuels. Biofuels displace gasoline and diesel fuel in vehicle fuel tanks, so the direct effect of additional biofuel production is to reduce the quantity of conventional fossil fuels consumed. By itself, this puts downward pressure on fossil fuel prices.

However, current biofuel production processes require extensive use of fossil fuels to grow the crops and operate biofuel processing plants. This may offset much of the fossil fuel savings, and limit the net effect of biofuel production on fossil fuel prices. The balance of these effects differs across types of biofuels, is difficult to measure, and remains controversial.

To get a flavor for the complexity of the issues, consider what happens when there is an increase in corn-based ethanol production. To produce more corn, farmers use more diesel fuel to operate the machinery used to grow and harvest the crop, and truckers use diesel fuel to transport corn from the farm to the ethanol plant and ethanol from the processing plant to locations where it is blended with gasoline. Natural gas is used to produce nitrogen fertilizer for corn production and as a fuel at ethanol plants. The ethanol is generally sold to the public in a 10-percent blend with gasoline.

The net result of all these changes is a reduction in oil-based gasoline consumption, but an increase in the consumption of diesel fuel and natural gas. Trying to estimate the overall effect of these changes on fuel prices is difficult. Gasoline and crude oil prices both are likely to be reduced, as the effect of reduced gasoline consumption is likely to outweigh the effect of increased diesel fuel consumption. Diesel fuel and natural gas prices, on the other hand, may actually increase. Short- and long-run effects may differ, as fuel producers and users adjust to changes in relative fuel prices.

The linkages between energy and food markets operate in both directions. Just as a change in the price of oil has an impact on markets for corn and other foods, a drought in the Midwest that reduces corn and ethanol production will have an impact on fuel markets. Biofuel production remains modest compared to total production of gasoline and diesel fuel. In 2008, for example, U.S. ethanol consumption was only about 7 percent of motor gasoline consumption by volume, and about 5 percent by energy content.[12] The effects of biofuel production on energy markets in general and gasoline markets in particular are likely to grow if biofuel production becomes a larger share of the total fuel supply.

The "Blend Wall" and Alternative Ethanol Blends

In the United States, most of the gasoline sold in 2009 contained 10 percent ethanol by volume. If ethanol production continues to expand, the market for 10 percent ethanol blends will soon be saturated. In the ethanol industry, this is often referred to as the *blend wall*, and many are concerned about the future of the industry once the blend wall is reached. The ethanol industry petitioned the Environmental Protection Agency to allow 15 percent ethanol blends to avert or at least delay the blend wall problem. If 15 percent blends are allowed, more ethanol can be consumed in conventional vehicles.

Some U.S. cars are equipped to use E-85, a fuel that contains up to 85 percent ethanol by volume, but only a few million such vehicles were on the road in 2009, and there were not many service stations that offered E-85. Even if these constraints are eased, few drivers will fill up their tanks with E-85 unless it is priced competitively with gasoline. Because a gallon of ethanol contains less energy than a gallon of gasoline, E-85 must sell at a significant discount to regular gasoline for it to deliver the same number of miles per dollar of fuel. This means that ethanol prices may have to decline relative to gasoline to encourage widespread adoption of E-85.

Brazil has long experience with ethanol fuels, and "flex-fuel" cars in Brazil are capable of running on 100 percent ethanol fuels or on gasoline blended with 20 percent to 25 percent ethanol. Brazilian drivers are very aware of the fuel economy they get with ethanol fuels, and will quickly adjust their fuel purchases depending on whether it is cheaper to buy pure ethanol or blended fuel. If ethanol is cheap relative to gasoline, Brazilian drivers fill up their flex-fuel cars with 100 percent ethanol. If ethanol is expensive relative to gasoline, they fill up with the blended fuel.

If the United States eventually increases its use of ethanol blended at rates higher than the current 10 percent, it is only likely to strengthen the relationship between oil, ethanol, and food prices. In 10 percent blends, some consumers may pay more for ethanol than its true energy value because it offers a higher octane fuel or simply because they have no choice in the matter. If higher blends become common, consumers are likely to be more sensitive to the relative prices of ethanol and regular gasoline. That will tend to keep ethanol and gasoline prices in a tighter relationship with one another. A tighter linkage between ethanol and gasoline prices is also likely to mean a tighter linkage between the prices of the agricultural products used in ethanol production and the price of petroleum.

Future Prospects

Crude oil and corn prices moved together more closely during the 2005–2009 period than in previous years. While this chapter has laid out reasons why food and energy markets are closely linked, a wide range of factors affect the price of food and a different but overlapping set of factors affect energy prices.

In the future, food and energy prices sometimes may move in opposite directions. Widespread crop failure can cause food prices to rise even if energy prices are falling. Government policies can severely weaken the linkages between energy and food markets. For example, the United States requires a minimum level of biofuel use. If crude oil prices are high, the demand for ethanol is likely to be strong enough that actual consumption will exceed this mandated minimum level. Thus, when oil prices are high, food and energy prices are likely to move together. When oil prices are low, biofuel consumption cannot fall below the legislated minimum.

If biofuel consumption is not allowed to change with fuel prices, one important linkage between energy prices and food prices is broken. There was evidence of this effect in the final months of 2008. Oil prices fell more sharply than corn prices, in part because biofuel use mandates did not let U.S. biofuel consumption and production fall as much as they otherwise would have in response to lower oil prices. The rebound in oil prices in 2009 did not cause a significant increase in grain prices, as there was no reason to expand biofuel production and use until ethanol was again priced competitively with gasoline.

Besides government policies, a number of other factors will affect the relationship between food and energy markets in the future. New technologies may make it possible to produce food in ways less reliant on fossil fuels. Technological breakthroughs could also make it possible to produce biofuels using raw materials that do not have such a direct effect on food prices as relying on grain, vegetable oil, and sugar. It is likely that energy and food markets will remain closely related to one another for years to come, even if the nature of the relationship evolves over time. At least for the next few years, sharp increases in energy prices are likely to result in sharp increases in food prices, just as we saw between 2005 and 2008.

Chapter 3

Policies Matter

Nearly 40 percent of the world's population earns a living by producing food, so government food policies matter—a lot.[1] Policies affect everything from basic agricultural research to the profitability of farming to whether the poor get enough food to survive. Almost all government food policies have some impact on food prices.

Some countries fix the price of basic foods. Tariffs drive up the price of imported food. Subsidies encourage increased food production and lower food prices. Biofuel policies mean crops are used to produce fuel rather than food, raising food prices. Food assistance programs make food more affordable for beneficiaries. Supply management programs pay farmers not to plant crops, reducing food production and raising food prices. Agricultural research can increase productivity and reduce food prices, or it can create alternative uses for agricultural products and raise food prices. Most countries simultaneously operate policies that reduce food prices and other policies that raise them.

Countries operate such contradictory food policies for a variety of political, social, and economic reasons. There is little agreement about what the purpose of food policies should be, and countries operate conflicting programs in pursuit of inconsistent objectives. A desirable objective of food policy may be to provide a safe and adequate supply of food at reasonable prices. However, trying to define "reasonable" food prices can lead to fundamental disagreements.

To a farmer, a reasonable price might be defined as a price high enough to cover production costs plus enough of a profit to allow the farmer to make a decent living. To a poor consumer, a reasonable price might be defined as a price low enough to ensure affordability of needed food with money left over to cover other basic needs. Quite often, farmers think that the market price is too low and seek policies that raise prices for the food they sell. Consumers may think market prices are too high and will seek policies that reduce the prices they pay for the food they buy.

To explain or even list all the food policies maintained by countries around the world would fill another book or even several volumes.[2] This chapter focuses on a few policies that had especially important effects on food prices between 2005 and 2009. Unlike traditional farm subsidy programs, many of these policies received little attention before 2007. Years of international trade negotiations have worked to establish a common set of rules governing a range of agricultural programs, but the negotiations have barely touched on some policies that have had profound effects on food prices in recent years.

When world food prices began to increase rapidly in 2007, a number of countries made policy changes to try to limit domestic food price inflation. Several traditional food exporting countries took steps to restrict food exports. Keeping more food at home increased domestic food supplies and lowered domestic prices. However, this also meant that less food was available to consumers in other countries. The result was higher prices for food importing countries.

At the same time, some food importing countries temporarily reduced tariffs and made other policy changes to encourage food imports. This had the effect of holding down food price inflation in these countries, but it also increased the overall world demand for imported food, which pushed up the price of food in world markets. In other words, both food exporters and food importers made policy changes that helped moderate domestic food price inflation in their own countries, but that had the effect of raising the prices at which food traded in international markets.

Given the wide range of conflicting food policies that exist in the world, it should not be surprising that the next rule of thumb is a little more nuanced than previous ones: *Government policies can both raise and lower food prices. Some policies that try to make domestic food prices more stable can make food prices in other countries more volatile.*

Government policies in one country have implications for farmers and food consumers in other countries. When the European Union or United States requires the use of biofuels, it raises the price of cereals and vegetable oil in Asia. When India restricts rice exports, it drives up rice prices in Africa and Latin America. It is precisely because food policies have cross-border implications that they have been a focus of controversy and a major sticking point in international trade negotiations.

The 2005–2009 Experience

A chorus of commentators has long criticized high-income countries for the effect their policies have on food prices in other countries. For decades, a common refrain has been that farm subsidies result in surpluses that depress food prices in the rest of the world. This gives farmers in high-income countries an unfair advantage over their counterparts in low-income countries that cannot afford to operate expensive subsidy programs. Artificially low food prices, it is argued, discourage the rural development that is essential in countries where a high proportion of the population is involved in farming. One stated objective of the last two rounds of international trade negotiations has been to limit the use of farm subsidies that depress world food prices.

Farm subsidies continue to be a major concern, but U.S. and E.U. biofuel policies were the focus of fierce debate in 2007 and 2008. Critics argued that the policies were a major factor behind the rapid increase in biofuel production, and that the soaring food prices of 2007 and early 2008 were a direct result. The increase in food prices was cited as a major factor behind the increase in world hunger, a cause of civil unrest in many countries, and a huge financial burden for food importing countries. Widespread calls were made for the United States and European Union to reduce or eliminate their support for biofuel production to moderate the increase in food prices. Jacques Diouf, Director of the U.N. Food and Agriculture Organization, said it is incomprehensible that "subsidies and protective tariff policies have the effect of diverting 100 million tons of cereals from human consumption, mostly to satisfy a thirst for vehicles."[3]

These complaints about the policies of high-income countries seem to be at odds with one another. Is the problem that high-income country policies reduce world food prices or that they raise world food prices? In reality, they do both, although the balance of effects changes over time. Low world food prices have negative effects on people who make a living by producing and selling food; high world food prices have negative effects on people who must purchase most or all the food they consume.

Some biofuel policies have been around for decades. Brazilian policies encouraged the initial investment in its ethanol industry, and the country has long required that gasoline be blended with ethanol. For many years, the United States has offered a subsidy that encourages domestic ethanol use and pushes up the price paid to ethanol producers. These preexisting policies would have been adequate to induce a substantial increase in biofuel production when oil prices rose from less than $30 per barrel in 2002 to more than $130 per barrel at the peak in mid-2008.

New policies in the European Union, the United States, and other countries provided additional incentives to increase biofuel production. The European Union set targets for the share of biofuels to be included in transportation fuels. E.U. countries were given some discretion in how these targets were to be met, but many countries chose to require that all fuel incorporate a specified proportion of biofuels. The resulting increase in demand for biofuels drove up biofuel prices in Europe. This made production of biodiesel and ethanol more profitable, resulting in a large increase in European production of biofuels. E.U. imports of biofuels also increased, so the E.U. policies had impacts on the biofuel sectors in other countries.

Unlike the United States, the European Union consumes more diesel fuel than gasoline. Consistent with this fuel mix, the initial emphasis in Europe was on increasing the use of biodiesel in blends with conventional diesel fuel. Biodiesel can be made from a range of vegetable oils and animal fats, but much of the initial investment in biodiesel production in Europe used rapeseed oil as the raw material, because rapeseed is the main oilseed grown in Europe. Soybean and palm oil are other vegetable oils used for biodiesel production.

The sharp increase in demand for rapeseed oil to make biodiesel was one of the main factors driving an increase in prices for rapeseed and other oils. Between the 2004/2005 and 2007/2008 marketing years, the prices of rapeseed oil, soybean oil, sunflower oil, palm oil, and corn oil all more than doubled.[4] Increasing food uses of vegetable oils in Asia and a number of other factors also played an important role in rising vegetable oil prices, but biodiesel use of vegetable oil was clearly a critical factor. For example, E.U. biodiesel use accounted for about 80 percent of the global increase in rapeseed oil use for all purposes between 2004/2005 and 2007/2008.[5]

In contrast to the European Union, the United States consumes a lot more gasoline than diesel fuel. In addition, the U.S. corn ethanol industry has a relatively long history—in 1985, more than 5 percent of all the corn used in the United States was processed by ethanol plants.[6] Government policies helped the corn ethanol industry get started, and policies have played an important role in the industry's expansion. Three major components of U.S. biofuel policy are subsidies for the production and use of ethanol, tariffs on ethanol imports, and mandates requiring minimum levels of biofuel use. Ethanol subsidies and tariffs have not increased in recent years—in fact, the most important ethanol subsidy was reduced on January 1, 2009. Biofuel use mandates were first introduced in legislation approved in 2005, and the minimum required levels of use have been increasing dramatically (see Table 3.1).

Table 3.1   *U.S. Biofuel Policies*

	2005	2007	2009
Ethanol tax credit/gallon	$0.51	$0.51	$0.45
Ethanol tariff/gallon	$0.54	$0.54	$0.54
Biodiesel credit/gallon	$1.00	$1.00	$1.00
Renewable Fuel Standard* (billion gallons)	None	4.70	11.10

*The Renewable Fuel Standard sets a minimum level of biofuel use over time. The 2007 Energy Independence and Security Act also sets mandates for use of particular types of biofuels.

These three policies all played a role in the expansion of the U.S. ethanol industry. The tax credit is available to those who blend ethanol with gasoline. The credit lets them offer ethanol producers a higher price, which encourages ethanol production, and it lets them charge a lower price to blended fuel consumers, encouraging ethanol consumption. The ethanol tariff makes Brazilian ethanol more expensive in the U.S. market. Limiting competition helps support domestic U.S. ethanol prices.[7] When oil prices rose between 2005 and 2008, prices paid to U.S. ethanol producers rose as well. The ethanol tax credit and the ethanol tariff meant that U.S. ethanol production was more profitable than it would have been in a policy-free world.

The Renewable Fuel Standard (RFS) sets minimum levels of U.S. biofuel use. Energy legislation passed in 2005 first established the

RFS, which initially was set at levels that proved to be far below actual levels of biofuel use. The sharp increase in oil prices and the phase-out of MTBE from the nation's fuel supply meant that there was more demand for ethanol than the RFS required. Because ethanol and biodiesel consumption exceeded the mandated amounts in 2006, 2007, and 2008, it is tempting to conclude that the RFS was not a major factor in the increase in biofuel production and food prices between 2005 and 2008.

The Energy Independence and Security Act (EISA), approved in late 2007, set far more ambitious goals. While the 2005 legislation set the RFS at levels that rose to 7.5 billion gallons, EISA set a 2022 target of 36 billion gallons of biofuel use. Recognizing concerns that excessive growth of ethanol production from corn could contribute to higher food prices, EISA set the maximum amount of corn-based ethanol that could count toward the RFS at 15 billion gallons in 2015 and subsequent years. The rest of the RFS is to be satisfied with "advanced biofuels" that do not utilize cornstarch in their production.

Even though U.S. biofuel consumption exceeded the RFS between 2005 and 2008, the RFS served as an insurance policy for the biofuel industry. Ethanol and biodiesel producers could be relatively certain that the RFS would put a floor beneath future growth in biofuel use, even if oil prices fell. The expectation of a rapidly growing RFS probably caused some ethanol and biodiesel plants to be constructed that would not have been built otherwise. The rapid growth in biofuel production capacity contributed to the increase in the use of corn and soybean oil to make ethanol and biodiesel, and also contributed to the rise in food prices.

There was no sudden reversal in biofuel policies in late 2008 that could explain the drop in food prices. The U.S. RFS remained in place, and the slight reduction in the U.S. ethanol tax credit only took effect in 2009. After much debate, the European Union confirmed its support for biofuels in a directive requiring increased use of biofuels and other sources of renewable energy. However, although there were no sharp changes in legislation or announced policy goals, political and regulatory uncertainty may have slowed new investment in biofuel production. For example, Texas Governor Rick Perry unsuccessfully sought a waiver in 2008 that would have had the effect of lowering the RFS. Rules to implement the 2007 EISA were still being written in 2009, and there were unresolved questions about how different types of biofuels would be treated under the regulations.

In addition to biofuel policies, another group of policies made an important contribution to the increase in world food prices in 2007 and 2008. Fear of food price inflation caused many countries to alter trade policies to discourage food exports or encourage food imports (see Table 3.2). This had the desired effect of increasing domestic food supplies and restraining domestic food price inflation in several countries, but it also had an important side effect. By reducing food available to other food importing countries, these policies set off a scramble for available supplies that drove up food prices in international markets.

The effects of these policy changes were perhaps most pernicious in the rice market. Only a small portion of the world's rice crosses country borders. In 2007/2008, for example, just 7 percent of world rice production was traded internationally.[8] India and Vietnam are normally two of the three largest exporters of rice in the world (Thailand is the leading exporter), so when both countries restricted rice exports, panic buying in world markets ensued.

The extent of the increase in world rice prices during the 2007/2008 marketing year is hard to explain without referring to the restrictions on rice trade. It is true that high prices for other grains put upward pressure on rice prices—if rice prices had remained low, some consumers would have switched from wheat- and corn-based foods to rice. However, a simple review of world rice supply and demand figures does not suggest circumstances that would normally

Table 3.2   *Policy Responses to Higher Food Prices in 2007 and 2008*

Country	Policy Changes
India	Banned exports of wheat and non-basmati rice
	Reduced import tariffs on wheat flour
China	Imposed a tax on grain exports
European Union	Suspended export subsidies on dairy products
	Reduced grain import tariffs
Russia	Raised export taxes on wheat
Indonesia	Imposed export tax on palm oil
	Reduced import tariffs on soybeans and wheat
Vietnam	Banned rice exports
Argentina	Raised export taxes on grains and oilseeds
Ukraine	Banned wheat exports

Source: Adapted from a USDA report by Ron Trostle, "Global Agricultural Supply and Demand: Factors Contributing to the Recent Increase in Food Commodity Prices," May 2008.

cause sharp price increases. World rice production actually exceeded rice consumption in 2007/2008, according to USDA estimates, and world stocks of rice were higher at the end of the year than they were at the beginning.[9] Without the restrictions on exports by India, Vietnam and other countries, the prices of rice traded in world markets would not have increased nearly as much.

Policy decisions also exaggerated swings in world dairy markets between 2005 and 2009. The European Union operates a complicated set of dairy policies, including quotas on how much milk farmers can market, support policies that put a floor under domestic market prices, and export subsidies to dispose of surpluses. Because of drought in Australia, strong demand growth in Asia and a variety of other factors, world dairy product prices rose sharply in 2007. To limit the increase in domestic European prices for milk and other dairy products, the European Union suspended dairy export subsidies to discourage exports. This further limited supplies in world markets, and caused world dairy product prices to rise even higher.

When world market prices for a number of food products fell in the final months of 2008 and early 2009, countries reversed at least some of the policies that had restricted exports and encouraged imports. The European Union reinstated dairy export subsidies and increased grain tariffs in response to lower world prices for dairy products and grains. Other countries lifted their bans on grain exports. Just as export restrictions and reduced import barriers had pushed world market prices higher in 2007 and early 2008, renewed export subsidies and increased import barriers pushed world market prices for food lower in late 2008 and early 2009.

Why the Story Is a Little More Complicated

The story of government policies and food prices is even more complicated than suggested so far. Consider the case of India. Not only did the country restrict grain exports in 2007 and 2008, but it also raised the minimum government prices paid to farmers for wheat and rice. Higher support prices encouraged Indian farmers to increase rice and wheat production in 2008. However, these support prices were not adjusted even after Indian grain supplies increased. As a result, domestic grain prices in India remained stubbornly high through the end of 2008, even though world market prices fell and Indian grain stocks reached the highest levels in years.[10]

Similar messy stories could be told about food policies in many countries. Most countries maintain a complex set of policies in pursuit of conflicting political and economic objectives. The United States simultaneously operates policies that encourage biofuel production and raise food prices and programs that subsidize food production and lower food prices.

How Do Biofuel Policies Affect Food Prices?

Biofuel support policies increase food prices. Most analysts would agree with that simple statement, but it would be much harder to get any type of consensus about how large the effects might be. To say that biofuel *production* had a major impact on food prices between 2005 and 2008 is not exactly the same thing as saying that biofuel *policies* had a large impact. The sharp increase in oil prices would have caused a significant increase in biofuel production between 2005 and 2008 even if countries had made no biofuel policy changes during that period. Removing all biofuel support policies would not have ended all biofuel production.

In a 2009 report, the Food and Agricultural Policy Research Institute at the University of Missouri (FAPRI-MU) estimates that removing the three major policies supporting the U.S. ethanol industry would reduce future U.S. ethanol production by an average of 36 percent.[11] Without tax credits, tariffs, or the RFS, the prices paid to ethanol producers would fall, new investment in corn-ethanol plants would grind to a halt, and some existing plants would shut down due to an inability to cover costs. This sharp reduction in ethanol production would have important market effects. For example, with less demand for corn for ethanol production, corn prices would fall. Lower corn prices would reduce a major cost faced by ethanol producers and allow the most efficient to remain in business, in spite of lower ethanol prices.

The potential impacts on food prices of ending U.S. ethanol support prices are significant. The FAPRI-MU study estimated that corn prices would fall by 13 percent, for example (see Table 3.3) Lower corn prices would encourage farmers to plant less corn and more soybeans and wheat, and encourage the use of more corn and less wheat and other cereals. These shifts in production and consumption would result in lower prices for competing crops. Lower prices for corn and other feeds, in turn, would reduce the cost of producing meat and milk. The result would be a slight increase in livestock production that would in turn result in a modest reduction in prices for cattle, hogs, chickens, and milk. These lower prices for farm products would, in turn, result in lower consumer food prices.

Table 3.3   *Impact of Removing U.S. Ethanol Policies on U.S. Crop and Livestock Prices*

Product	Percentage Change
Corn	-13.1
Wheat	-7.4
Soybeans	-5.6
Cattle	-1.6
Hogs	-4.1
Chickens	-3.3
Milk	-1.3

Note: Estimates are average impacts over an 8-year period if the ethanol tax credit, the ethanol tariff, and the Renewable Fuel Standard are eliminated.

Source: FAPRI-MU report #04-09, "Effects of Selected U.S. Ethanol Policy Options."

In a high-income country like the United States, the proportional impact on consumer food prices of eliminating ethanol support policies would be fairly small. In the FAPRI-MU study, for example, the estimated change in U.S. consumer food expenditures is less than one percent. This modest effect occurs because the cost of raw farm

commodities is only a small fraction of the value of the food consumers buy in grocery stores and restaurants. In a low-income country where corn, wheat and other basic grains account for a significant
share of food purchases, these effects would be much larger.

The current mix of U.S. ethanol support policies makes for a very
complicated relationship between ethanol and gasoline markets.
When oil and gasoline prices are very high, as they were in mid-2008,
the demand for ethanol is strong, as people seek a cheaper alternative
to regular gasoline. This results in higher ethanol prices than when
gasoline prices are low. The ethanol tax credit has the effect of further
pushing up the price of ethanol to producers while holding down the
price of ethanol to consumers. Thus, when oil prices are high, the
ethanol tax credit can encourage more ethanol production and use,
which in turn causes more corn use and higher food prices.

From 2005 to 2008, U.S. ethanol production and consumption
were more than sufficient to satisfy requirements of the RFS. The
combination of rising oil prices and maintenance of the tax credit and
import tariff were sufficient to cause U.S. ethanol production to
expand rapidly. When oil prices fell sharply in the final months of
2008, the picture changed. Lower gasoline prices meant ethanol was
less competitive as a fuel, even with the tax credit in place. Ethanol
prices fell to levels where many producers could no longer cover their
costs, and several plants shut down.

Suddenly, the RFS became very relevant to biofuel markets after
having been little more than an insurance policy for biofuel producers
in previous years. By the final months of 2008, it appeared likely that
the 2009 RFS would be "binding," meaning that firms would only
choose to use the quantities of ethanol and biodiesel that the law
required, as there was no longer an economic incentive to use biofuel in excess of the RFS. Biofuel suppliers had to be paid a high enough
price to convince them to produce the required quantities of ethanol
and biodiesel, regardless of conditions in the gasoline and diesel fuel

markets. This meant that the previous close connection between prices in petroleum and biofuel markets was broken, or at least weakened. Gasoline and diesel fuel blenders started paying each other for the right *not* to use biofuels, under a trading system set up under the 2005 energy bill.

Policies strongly affect the relationship between energy and food prices. If there were no biofuel support policies, the price of oil would effectively set a floor under food prices. If grain, sugar, and vegetable oil prices were too low relative to petroleum prices for an extended period of time, biofuel producers would make so much money that firms would invest in new plants. Biofuel production would expand until the resulting increase in farm product prices meant that biofuel plants were no longer making unusually large profits.

Biofuel subsidies like the U.S. ethanol tax credit do not change this fundamental relationship. However, by pushing up prices paid to biofuel producers relative to the price of oil, they result in greater biofuel production and higher food prices than would otherwise occur. Energy and agricultural markets remain linked, but the average price of food is higher for any given oil price. An increase in oil prices eventually results in higher prices for corn, sugar, vegetable oil, and other foods, just as it would in the absence of the subsidy.

However, if low oil prices, a small corn crop, or other factors mean that biofuel consumption falls to the levels required by the RFS, the relationship between energy and agricultural markets changes dramatically. No longer do changes in oil prices necessarily translate into changes in food prices, at least not because of biofuels. To satisfy the RFS, firms will only pay ethanol and biodiesel producers the price necessary to convince them to supply the required quantities of biofuels. That price will not change, at least not very much, depending on the price of oil, gasoline, and diesel fuel. Thus the current policy mix in the United States means that the linkage between food and fuel market prices is likely to be very strong when oil prices are high, but may be very weak when oil prices are low.

Food Policies in a Global Context

Biofuel policies and measures countries took to reduce domestic food price inflation were especially important in explaining food price developments between 2005 and 2009. This does not mean, of course, that other government policies do not also have very important effects on food markets. Most of these other policies, however, either have been in place for many years or they did not contribute much to the observed changes in food prices in recent years.

High-income countries tend to operate policies that provide support to domestic farmers, usually at the expense of either taxpayers or consumers. The Organization for Economic Cooperation and Development (OECD) estimates the overall value of support to farmers in high-income countries in both absolute terms and as a share of the value of farm receipts from market sales and government farm subsidies (Table 3.4). The calculations are both complex and controversial; some countries argue that the report is misleading and includes flawed estimates. Other measures would change the rankings. For example the European Union has pointed out that subsidies per farm are greater in the United States than in the European Union.

Even after taking all of those qualifications into account, the estimates in Table 3.4 make a couple of important points. First, government policies are responsible for a large share of farm income in many countries. Across all OECD countries, government subsidies and policies that keep domestic prices above world market levels account for

Table 3.4   *OECD Producer Support Estimates, as a
Share of Farm Receipts, 2006–2008*

Country	Percent
South Korea	61
Japan	49
European Union	27
OECD average	23
Canada	18
United States	10
Australia	6
New Zealand	1

Note: Estimates reflect the value to farmers of government policies (both direct subsidies and policies that support domestic prices above levels prevailing in world markets), divided by the total farm receipts from sales and government payments.

Source: OECD, "Agricultural Policies in OECD Countries: Monitoring and Evaluation 2009."

about one-fourth of total farm receipts. Second, government support is much greater in some countries than in others. Without arguing about the precise rankings, there is clearly a major difference between the policies of countries such as Australia and New Zealand that do little to subsidize domestic farmers and of countries such as Japan and those in the European Union where support measures make a critical contribution to the income of farmers.

What effect do all these policies have on food prices? Trade policies, farm subsidies, food assistance programs, and other food policies all have distinct effects.

Trade Policies

Many countries impose tariffs on food imports from other countries. Tariffs drive a wedge between food prices in exporting and importing countries. When an importer puts a tariff in place, it drives up the price of food in the importing country and drives down the price of food in the exporting country. When the United States imposes a large tariff on sugar imports from Brazil, for example, it results in higher U.S. sugar prices and lower prices for Brazilian sugar in other markets. Countries also restrict imports in other ways. Countries may refuse to import certain products from another country if they are concerned about the transmission of human, plant, or animal diseases. These policies tend to increase food prices in the country restricting imports and reduce food prices in the country that would like to export.

Some countries have used export subsidies to dispose of food surpluses. These subsidies let buyers in importing countries obtain food at a lower price than would otherwise be available, and sometimes even lower than prices in the exporting country. Such policies prop up food prices in the country offering the export subsidy but reduce food prices in the importing country. For other exporters to compete with the subsidizing country, they must either offer similar subsidies or accept a lower price for the food they sell. Many countries are especially opposed to export subsidies, and their elimination has been a goal of international trade negotiations. However, there have been many arguments about how to define export subsidies. For example, where should one draw the line between legitimate food aid programs intended to provide humanitarian assistance and export subsidies intended to dispose of domestic surpluses?

Subsidies and Other Programs Intended to Benefit Farmers

Many high-income countries write government checks to farmers. Much of the debate about 2008 U.S. farm legislation and recent reforms of the E.U. Common Agricultural Policy was about the rules that determine which farmers get paid how much under what circumstances. Subsidies that are directly tied to how much a farmer produces or sells are especially likely to encourage farmers to produce more. For example, the United States has operated a policy known as the "marketing loan program" that pays a subsidy for every pound or bushel produced when market prices are below a trigger level. When grain and oilseed prices are as high as they have been since 2006, the marketing loan program does not make any payments to farmers of those crops. In general, subsidies tied to production encourage food production and reduce food prices. Farmers in low-income countries that cannot afford to operate such policies complain when high-income countries offer such subsidies and depress world food prices.

Some farm subsidies are paid in ways not tied directly to current production levels. For example, both the United States and the European Union operate programs that make billions of dollars of payments to farmers that are based on what they produced on their farms in the past, but not on what they produce today. The U.S. direct payment program makes payments tied to the crops planted on a farm before 2001 and the yields obtained on that farm prior to 1985. The E.U. single farm payment operates differently in various E.U. countries, but in no case is the payment tied to the current mix of crops grown on a farm. These policies can transfer a lot of money from taxpayers to farmers, but they may not have a very large effect on what a farmer chooses to produce. Economists tend to agree that a tax dollar spent on subsidies not tied to current production probably has a smaller impact on food prices than a dollar spent on subsidies that are directly tied to current food production choices.

Droughts, floods, and other natural disasters reduce crop yields and farm income and raise food prices. Many countries provide special assistance to farmers when natural disasters strike, and several offer subsidized crop insurance programs. In the United States, for example, the federal government subsidizes the premiums paid by farmers for crop insurance policies provided by private companies, and taxpayers absorb most of the losses when there is a widespread crop failure. These programs have mixed effects on food production and prices. On the one hand, they provide an additional subsidy, which can encourage increased food production; on the other hand, they may discourage some producers from taking appropriate steps to reduce the likelihood of crop losses.

Countries may support the prices of key food products. In addition to using border measures such as export subsidies or tariffs, they may provide for government purchases of food at predetermined prices. If the government is willing to buy whatever food is offered to it at a given price, it is very difficult for market prices to ever fall very far below the support price. The challenge with such policies is deciding what to do with the surpluses that governments can accumulate if production exceeds consumption at the support price.

Some countries operate supply management programs in conjunction with price supports. For example, the European Union has long operated a very strict milk quota program. A price support is set for various dairy products, and each producer is only allowed to sell a fixed amount of milk. If the milk quota is set properly, there is no reason for surpluses to develop and milk prices are likely to stay at or above the price support level. The trade-off is that farmers are not free to produce as much as they would like, at least not without buying the right to produce more from another farmer who is willing to cut production. The E.U. milk quota program is scheduled to end in a few years. Other supply management policies include programs that require or pay farmers to idle farmland. These programs are less common now than they were previously; the United States has not required farmers to set aside cropland to get basic farm program benefits since 1996. In general, supply management policies are intended to restrict food supplies and raise food prices.

Many countries provide farm credit services. Public banks and credit agencies make loans to farmers at interest rates below commercial levels. Special tax provisions reduce the net cost to farmers of new investments. When these programs make it easier for farmers to make worthwhile investments, they can increase farm productivity and lower food prices. However, in other cases programs can steer investment into areas that do little or nothing to increase food production.

Another common policy is to subsidize fertilizer, fuel, or other farm production inputs. In developing countries with many small farmers, it is often easier for governments to encourage food production by holding down the cost of key inputs rather than providing cash subsidies to millions of farmers. Like farm credit programs, input subsidies result in higher food production and lower food prices. But like credit programs, they can sometimes divert resources away from their best uses, and excess use of some production inputs can harm the environment.

Programs Targeted at Food Consumers

Countries operate international food aid programs to provide humanitarian assistance and to dispose of domestic food surpluses. In general, such policies tend to increase food supplies and reduce food prices in the recipient countries, but provide at least some modest support to food prices in the donor country. The food price impacts depend critically on how the programs are designed and operated. For example, it makes a difference whether the food provided is purchased in the donor country or in the region where the recipients live. In the former case, food prices in the recipient country are likely to fall; in the latter case, they are likely to increase.

Many countries maintain domestic food assistance programs to reduce the cost of food to at least some low-income people. In India, this has been done by offering reduced-price food in shops located in poor neighborhoods. In the United States, the Supplemental Nutrition Assistance Program (SNAP, formerly known as the food stamp program) offers monthly benefits to low-income families tied to the cost of a basket of basic and inexpensive foods. In fiscal year 2008, federal spending on the SNAP program totaled $39 billion, making it far larger than all the farm subsidy programs operated by the U.S. Department of Agriculture combined.[12] Food assistance programs provide additional resources to low-income families and increase consumption of some foods. This also contributes to modest increases in food prices for other consumers.

To ensure food safety, governments require meat inspection, test agricultural chemicals, ban practices that are judged likely to endanger human or animal health, and set other rules for how food is produced and sold. These policies help ensure a safe and healthy food supply, but critics argue that many existing policies are inadequate or misguided. Some of these policies impose additional costs on food producers and result in an increase in food prices.

Other Policies Affecting the Food Sector

Several countries maintain public stocks of grains or other foods. Sometimes this is done in conjunction with price support programs. Countries may acquire food when market prices fall to or below price support levels, and then store the food until prices increase or they determine some other way to dispose of the stocks. In the past, the United States and the European Union held grain surplus stocks in government storage as a by-product of price support programs. The United States has made policy changes that make it unlikely that it will accumulate large public food stocks in the future. China was another country that once held large government stocks of grain, but those were reduced sharply by 2007. Government stock programs are expensive to maintain, so it is easy to understand why many countries chose to reduce government food stocks. However, it does mean that less of a buffer is available to moderate food price increases when there is an unexpected reduction in food production or an unexpected surge in demand, as occurred between 2005 and 2008.

Governments around the world fund both basic and applied agricultural research. Some of this research develops new seeds and production techniques intended to help farmers increase production. When this research succeeds, the result is more food production and lower food prices. Other research develops new uses for agricultural products, such as biofuels. When this research is successful, the result is that less agricultural production is available for food uses, and food prices increase. In addition to public research, a lot of agricultural research is done by seed companies, agricultural chemical providers, machinery manufacturers, and other private firms. Public policies can restrict or encourage various types of agricultural research, whether private biotechnology research or public research on organic farming methods. Policy choices about the types of research to encourage, discourage, or prohibit all have implications for food production and prices.

Some conservation programs help farmers protect and better use natural resources, with positive short- and long-run effects on food production. Policies intended to reduce soil erosion and improve the use of irrigation water, for example, can increase food production and lower food prices; but some conservation policies prohibit the use of parks and other environmentally sensitive lands for food production or they pay farmers to idle cropland. For example, the U.S. conservation reserve program pays farmers to idle land for ten years to reduce soil erosion, improve water quality, and enhance wildlife habitat. In June 2009, 34 million acres were enrolled in the conservation reserve. This compares to approximately 316 million acres devoted to U.S. production of 13 major field crops and hay.[13] These programs can have very important environmental benefits, but by reducing food production, they also cause higher food prices.

The European Union and other countries have established rules to protect the welfare of livestock and poultry. Like food safety policies, animal welfare rules place restrictions on how farmers operate. The result can be higher production costs and higher food prices. As with conservation programs that take land out of production or food safety rules, there are real costs to go along with any benefits.

This list is far from complete, but it does illustrate the wide range of food policies that countries maintain and the effects they can have on food prices. A serious point of contention has been the distribution of farm program benefits. Many if not most farm programs provide support to farmers in ways that are somehow tied to current or past levels of production. This is true not just of programs that pay direct subsidies to farmers, but also of import tariffs, export subsidies, price supports, and other measures that prop up the price of domestic farm products. As a result, the larger the farm, the larger are the government farm program benefits it receives. It is often argued that taxpayers should not provide large subsidies to the biggest farms, and farm legislation in some countries includes various types of limits on who can receive how much in farm program subsidies.

Much of the debate about food policies focuses on things that do not have large impacts on food prices. For example, a lot of farm subsidy programs, especially those not tied to current production levels, significantly impact the income of farm families and landowners, but probably have relatively little impact on food production and prices. Policies that historically received little attention can actually have much larger impacts on food prices than policies that have been the focus of intense public debate.

Future Policy Effects on Food Prices

All the policies discussed above affect food prices. If the experience of 2005 to 2009 is any guide, food prices will also be affected by policies not yet on the radar screen. Consider, for example, concerns about global warming and policy measures that could try to reduce future emissions of greenhouse gases. Agricultural production is both an important emitter of greenhouse gases and an important means of sequestering carbon. Agricultural use of fuel and fertilizer results in carbon emissions, and cows and rice production are important sources of greenhouse gases, too. Some crop production practices, on the other hand, can lock up more carbon in the soil, certain types of biofuel production can reduce net carbon emissions compared to the use of fossil fuels, and planting trees on farms can also increase carbon sequestration.

Legislation to reduce greenhouse gas emissions could have important impacts on food production. If the result is higher prices for fuel and fertilizer, farm production costs will increase. If increased incentives are offered for planting trees, some land will be diverted from production of crops and livestock to forestry uses. If incentives are provided to encourage biofuel production or the use of biomass to generate electricity, less land will be available for other agricultural use. All these factors have the potential to reduce food production and raise food prices. Offsetting these concerns is the potential long-term benefit of mitigating climate change, which could be very important for food production and prices around the world.

The future of food policy is still to be determined. Some policy choices are made at the local level—should public funds be used to support farmers markets and community gardens? Most policy choices are made at the national level—should policies support biofuel production? Other policy choices are made in international trade negotiations—should countries agree to limit certain types of farm subsidies? This book is not intended to provide a particular set of policy prescriptions regarding these and other questions, but it is intended to help readers have some of the information they need to join the debate.

Chapter 4

Rain and Grain

Farmers say that "rain makes grain," and it is hard to exaggerate the effect that weather has on food production and prices. The price of a loaf of bread in Boston or a bowl of rice in Beijing may depend on a complex set of economic forces that affect global food supply and demand, but it also depends critically on the weather.

Crop production falls and food prices rise when it does not rain the right amount, in the right place, at the right time. Drought in Kansas, a failed monsoon in India, or floods in Germany can all reduce crop production and drive up food prices. If unfavorable weather affects a small area, it may be devastating to local farmers but have little impact on global food markets. A widespread drought in a key production region can have drive up food prices on the other side of the world.

Some years, everything goes right. Timely rains and days that are neither too hot nor too cold can help crops develop to their full potential. The resulting increase in crop supplies puts downward pressure on food prices. Global demand for food usually does not change very much from one year to the next. Weather-induced changes in crop supplies disrupt the balance between food supply and demand, and can cause large swings in food prices. Thus, another rule of thumb: *Food prices rise when adverse weather reduces crop yields and fall when favorable weather results in bumper crops.*

For several thousand years, grain producers have understood how important the weather is in determining annual harvests. Irrigation and a wide range of other technologies have been developed to mitigate the effects of unfavorable weather on crop production. For example, a high proportion of the world's rice is grown on irrigated land, so that the crop has the proper amount of moisture at the right time. This has increased rice yields and made them much less variable than yields for many other crops that rely more on uncertain rainfall.

Most of the world's cropland is not irrigated because it is impractical or unnecessary. It is a lot easier to irrigate flat lands near a major river than it is a steep hillside located far from the closest source of fresh water. In much of the world, normal rainfall is adequate to grow crops profitably, and the cost of installing and operating an irrigation system exceeds the benefits. On nonirrigated cropland, the connection between rain and grain is fairly direct—it is not possible for crops to attain their maximum yields without adequate precipitation, but too much rain at the wrong time may reduce yields. Even on irrigated cropland, a particularly bad drought reduces the amount of water available for irrigation, with devastating effects on crop production.

A range of other factors affects crop yields. Some soils are far more suited to crop production than others. Seed choice, fertilization, tillage, pest and weed control, and production practices come into play. These are all important factors in explaining the average *level* of crop yields in a given area, but they tend not to change much from one year to the next. Large year-to-year *changes* in crop yields cannot be explained by factors that remain constant or change only slowly over time.

In most of the world, the weather is the main reason why crop yields increase or decrease from one year to the next. Annual precipitation is a key variable, but it matters when it rains as well. Too much rain at planting time can make it impossible to get a crop in the ground. Too little rain at key stages of crop development is more devastating than if the same weather pattern occurred just a few weeks earlier or later. Temperature matters, too. An ill-timed frost can kill a young plant or keep a crop from reaching full maturity and maximum yields. Excessive heat can put great stress on a plant, especially when rainfall is inadequate.

Each crop in each location has its own critical periods for both rainfall and temperature. Grains and oilseeds grown in North America and Europe are generally planted and harvested about six months before the same crops grown in Australia and Argentina, simply because of the hemispheric difference in the seasons. Even on a particular farm, each crop has its own growing season. In Missouri, for example, a single farm may have winter wheat seeded in the fall, corn planted in May and soybeans planted in June. Excessive rain in May can make it difficult for farmers to plant corn in a timely manner and may force them to switch to soybeans or another crop with a different growing season.

Livestock and poultry are also affected by weather conditions. Extreme weather endangers animal health, increasing mortality and reducing the ability of animals to gain weight, cows to produce milk, and chickens to lay eggs. Drought does not just affect production of grain and other major field crops; it also reduces forage availability from pastureland, directly affecting cattle and sheep diets.

Key players in world food markets recognize the link between the weather and crop yields. Traders on futures markets buy and sell contracts for future delivery of grains, oilseeds, and other products. These traders revise their estimates of the balance between food supply and demand with every new piece of information, and adjust what they are willing to pay or offer for a futures contract. Therefore, prices in futures markets rise and fall in response to actual and forecast weather conditions; traders do not wait for a crop to be harvested to guess how large it is. Most of the time, the price a farmer can get in local cash markets increases or decreases in line with futures prices.

A running joke among food market analysts is that futures market prices are strongly affected by the weather in downtown Chicago, where the largest futures market exchanges are located. If a futures market trader looks out his window in July and sees it is raining, he will sell corn futures, driving down the price. In reality, of course, traders recognize the interconnected nature of world commodity markets, and will not just look out the window but at weather conditions and forecasts in all the other major growing regions around the world. The price a farmer in Iowa can get for his corn today depends on the forecast for rain in Illinois or China or France. If the weather forecast changes, the futures price of corn also changes, even before the first drop of rain falls or fails to fall.

The 2005–2009 Experience

The weather played an important role in the rise and fall of food prices in recent years. In 2004, near-perfect weather led to record grain crops in the United States, the E.U., and the world as a whole. In the United States, for example, the 2004 corn yield per acre not only set a record, but it broke the previous record by almost 13 percent. World cereal production increased by almost 10 percent, and almost the entire increase was explained by higher yields per acre. In spite of continued increases in global grain consumption, this sharp increase in production made it possible to rebuild global grain stocks after years of decline.[1]

This large supply of grain put downward pressure on food prices. U.S. export prices for corn dropped below $100 per ton in September 2004, and remained low over most of the next two years as world markets responded to a glut of grain. Wheat prices also declined in late 2004 and were slow to recover. The exception to this general pattern was rice, where world average yields were well below the long-term trend for three straight years from 2002 to 2004.[2] However, even this exception helps prove the point about the relationship between crop yields and prices. Reduced rice yields contributed to a drawdown of global rice stocks and an increase in the price at which rice traded in international markets.[3]

After the bumper crop of 2004, more normal weather resulted in 2005 world cereal yields that were very close to the long-term trend. This helped contribute to a period when world grain prices in particular and food prices in general were relatively stable. U.S. consumer food prices rose by 2.4 percent in 2005 and again in 2006, comparable to the general rate of consumer price inflation.

Developments in three major grain exporters demonstrate the effect of weather on food prices. In response to generally favorable weather, total grain production in the E.U., Ukraine, and Australia reached record levels in 2004 (see Figure 4.1). Drought in Australia and much of Europe sharply reduced grain yields in 2006 and 2007. Total grain production in these exporters declined by 77 million metric tons (20 percent) between 2004 in 2007. Even relative to world cereal production and consumption of about 2 billion metric tons, that is a very sizable decline, large enough to put strong upward pressure on grain prices (see Figure 4.2).

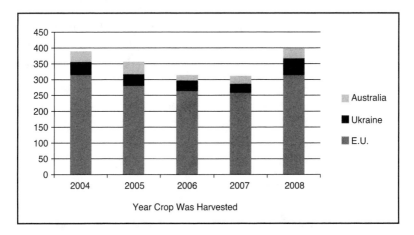

Figure 4.1 *Grain production in three key exporters, million metric tons*

Source: Author calculations based on the USDA's online data set, "Production, Supply and Distribution Online," September 2009.

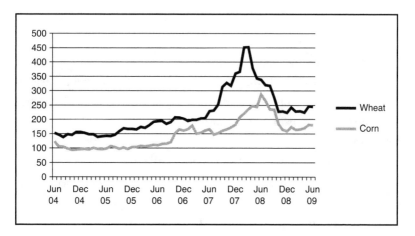

Figure 4.2 *U.S. grain export prices, dollars per metric ton*

Source: Monthly price data from the USDA's Economic Research Service. The wheat price is for #1 hard red winter wheat in Kansas City, and the corn price is for #2 yellow corn at U.S. gulf ports.

The decline in production in the E.U., Ukraine, and Australia was important precisely because these countries are normally major grain exporters. Ukraine and Australia reduced their grain exports in response to reduced production, and the European Union not only reduced its grain exports but it actually imported significant amounts of grain in 2007/2008. The 77 million metric ton decline in cereal production in three key exporters translated into 35 million metric tons less grain available to consumers in other countries. The rest of the change in production was absorbed in domestic markets by reducing consumption and carryover stocks.

So how big of a deal is a 35 million metric ton decline in cereal net exports? World cereal trade was about 275 million metric tons in the 2007/2008 marketing year, so the reduction in exports by the E.U., Ukraine, and Australia is equivalent to about 13 percent of all the grain traded in world markets. By almost any measure, that is a very significant sum.

Another way to put the decline into perspective is to examine what happened to cereal exports by the United States over the same 2004–2007 period. The United States has been the world's largest cereal exporter by far. Between 2004/2005 and 2007/2008, U.S. cereal net exports increased by 21 million metric tons. In other words, the increase in U.S. cereal exports offset some, but not all, of the decline in exports by the E.U., Ukraine, and Australia.

Many competing explanations have been offered for the increase in U.S. cereal exports over the 2004–2007 period, and most of the explanations focus on forces that increased global demand for cereals and other food products. However, it is clear that crop supplies were also an important part of the story. The changes in world cereal trade between 2004 and 2007 suggest that U.S. exports increased largely to fill the hole left by reduced exports from major competitors. That makes it hard to argue that the increase in world cereal prices was *only* a function of strong global demand for grain. If it were, one would not have expected to see reduced foreign sales by several major exporters.

Many of the same forces that caused food prices to increase between 2005 and early 2008 reversed course, and the result was lower food prices in the final months of 2008. This is certainly true in the case of cereal production and trade by the E.U., Ukraine, and Australia. Growing conditions were much better in all three exporters in 2008, and the result was a sharp increase in cereal production. The year-over-year increase in cereal production by the three exporters between 2007 and 2008 was about 87 million metric tons.[4] Most of this increase in production was reflected in an increase in cereal exports.

This large increase in E.U., Ukrainian, and Australian cereal production and exports put severe downward pressure on world cereal market prices. Increased exports by these three competitors reduced the demand for cereal exports from the United States. The reduction in U.S. cereal exports in 2008/2009 was less than the increase in exports by the three competitors. Once again, weather-induced variation in crop supplies was a major cause of shifts in U.S. trade.

In summary, bad weather in 2006 and 2007 in key countries reduced cereal production and limited exports. These reduced supplies on global markets contributed to the increase in food prices between 2005 and early 2008. Once it became clear that favorable weather would result in much greater cereal production in 2008, prices fell.

Why the Story Is a Little More Complicated

The story is a little too simple. Although it is true that weather in a few countries played an important role in food price developments during the 2005–2008 period, the full story requires further explanation.

Cherry Picking

In any given year, good weather will cause good crops in some regions, and bad weather will cause poor crops in other regions. The world average cereal yield in 2007 was in line with the historical trend.[5] While yields in the E.U., Ukraine, and Australia were below normal, this was offset by better-than-average yields in other countries. China and India, for example, had good rice yields in 2007, and Brazilian corn yields reached record levels.

It does not seem fair to blame high food prices in 2007 and early 2008 on bad crop yields when world-average yields in 2007 were about what one would have expected with average growing conditions. The countries that experienced good yields in 2007 should have been able to make up for reduced supplies from the countries that had below-average yields. That this did not occur suggests that global averages do not tell the whole story; it matters where food production expands and contracts. In contrast, 2008 world cereal yields were above the long-term trend, and this certainly contributed to the decline in crop prices.

Production, Area, and Yields

Annual changes in crop production are not simply a function of crop yields per acre or hectare. Farmers adjust the amount of land they devote to crop production in general and to the production of particular crops. In 2007, for example, U.S. farmers responded to price signals by shifting a lot of land into corn production, largely at the expense of soybean area, but also by slightly increasing the total amount of land used for crop production.

In the case of the selected exporters, most of the observed change in production could be attributed to changes in yields rather than changes in area. Between 2004 and 2007, for example, the total cereal area harvested in the E.U., Ukraine, and Australia declined by 5 percent while yields per harvested hectare declined by 16 percent. Between 2007 and 2008, the three exporters increased cereal area harvested by 6 percent and yields increased by 20 percent. The increase in area in 2008 could be attributed in part to responses by both farmers and governments to high crop prices.

Weather, Yields, and Area

Annual changes in crop yields are not simply a function of the weather. Farmers can and do make management changes based on economic incentives. Higher cereal prices, for example, may encourage farmers to increase the use of fertilizer and other inputs to try to maximize returns. How farmers choose to combat weeds, insect pests, and plant diseases depends on the economic costs and benefits of various practices, each of which has implications for crop yields.

Just how much effect these annual management decisions have on crop yields in a particular year is controversial. One line of thought is that such effects are likely to be modest in the short run, as production practices tend not to change very much from one year to the next, even when crop and input prices change. In the long run, yields could be much more responsive to prices as new technologies are developed and disseminated in response to economic incentives. For example, it takes several years to develop a new type of seed and bring it to the marketplace. Thus, the weather may be the primary factor determining annual variation in crop yields, even if crop and input prices, public and private research investments, and a wide variety of other factors affect longer-term growth rates.

Weather affects the area devoted to crop production as well as the yield per harvested hectare. Springtime floods can make it impossible for farmers to plant the intended crop. Crop failure due to drought or pests may mean that land that is planted is never harvested. Some of the reduction in recorded Australian cereal area harvested in 2006 and 2007 was a direct result of drought conditions.

Location and Policies

When yields increase or decrease in a country that is open to world trade, the effects are felt around the world. Changes in yields in major trading countries are important precisely because they are major trading countries. When a country such as Australia has a drought, domestic grain consumption in Australia does not change very much, but Australian grain exports decline sharply. This reduction in Australian exports raises the prices that cereal importers pay and the prices that competing exporters can obtain. In other words, all countries open to cereal trade absorb part of the impact of an Australian drought.

In contrast, consider the case of a country isolated from world markets by government restrictions on trade or high transportation costs caused by poor roads and geographic remoteness. When that country suffers a drought, the effects can be devastating for the local population. The available food supply is reduced, which can result in dramatic increases in food prices and hunger. Because the country's cereal trade with the rest of the world does not change, there is no reason for cereal prices in other countries to change.

This illustrates an important trade-off in the debate over food security. Countries that are open to trade are affected by all the factors affecting food supply and demand in all the other trading countries. Thus, much of the volatility in domestic food prices will originate in other countries. On the other hand, when such a country suffers a drought or other unexpected reduction in the domestic food supply, the country's ability to access world markets provides a buffer that can limit the impact on domestic food prices. In contrast, a country that avidly pursues a self-sufficiency policy will protect itself from food price volatility that originates in other countries, but may be subject to sharply higher food prices when there is a domestic crop shortfall.

Farm Commodity Prices

Wheat is not corn, grains are not oilseeds, and feeds are not livestock, but they are all related. The main crop directly affected by unfavorable weather in the E.U., Ukraine, and Australia in 2007 was wheat. As concerns about wheat supplies increased, so did wheat prices. Even if poor weather had not affected yields of any other crops, the increase in wheat prices would have had at least some ripple effects across other farm commodities. In Figure 2.2, note that wheat prices increased earlier and more than corn prices, but the two prices moved in tandem from June 2008 to June 2009.

When wheat prices increase, at least some users of wheat try to find cheaper alternatives. In some cases, there may be no good options; it is difficult to replace wheat flour in bakery products, for example, so users simply have to pay the higher price. On the other hand, livestock producers will quickly adjust feed rations to minimize costs, so when wheat prices increase, they use less wheat and more corn. This increase in the use of corn in feed, in turn, results in higher corn prices. Market developments in 2007 are consistent with this story; prices for the types of wheat that cannot be easily replaced rose to dizzying heights, but the prices of feed-quality wheat never became totally divorced from prices for corn and other grains fed to livestock.

In choosing which crops to plant, farmers pay close attention to the relative prices of alternative crops. If wheat prices rise more than prices for other crops, farmers will plant more wheat and less corn, soybeans, or barley. As markets anticipate reduced production of these other crops, their prices will also rise. Thus an increase in wheat prices will eventually translate into at least some increase in prices for a wide range of other crops, due to substitution effects in both demand and supply.

Higher feed prices reduce the profitability of meat, poultry and milk production. Some livestock producers scale back, and this eventually results in less meat and milk production and higher prices. How long this takes to play out depends in part on some basic biology. It only takes a few weeks from the time an egg hatches until a chicken is ready for slaughter, so poultry production and prices respond rapidly to changes in feed prices. At the other extreme, it can take two years or more from the time a cow is bred to the time a steer is ready for slaughter, so it takes much longer for the effects of higher feed prices to be fully reflected in beef production and prices.

Commodity Prices and Food Prices

The effect of higher farm commodity prices on consumer food prices varies across food items. Changes in wheat prices have small proportional impacts on the cost of producing a box of breakfast cereal or a loaf of bread. Even a large increase in grain prices is likely to have only modest impacts on consumer food prices in high-income countries where most of the cost of producing food occurs after commodities leave the farm.

In low-income countries where many consumers rely on basic staples, the same increase in farm commodity prices may have a much larger proportional impact on consumer food prices than it does in high-income countries. Thus a drought in Australia may result in a smaller percentage increase in consumer food prices in Australia than in some low-income wheat-importing countries on the other side of the world.

Weather and Managing the Food Supply Chain

Unpredictable weather can make it difficult to manage the supply chains that result in consumer-ready foods. This is easiest to see in the case of the local farmer's market. Suppose frost wipes out the local strawberry crop. Even consumers willing to pay a high premium for fresh local strawberries will find none available at the farmer's market. Some enterprising vendors might try to bring in some strawberries from a region not affected by the frost. However, those imported strawberries are likely to be more expensive, both because of transportation costs and because the local crop failure may make a significant dent in total regional strawberry supplies. Furthermore, they will not be the local strawberries some consumers prefer.

Now consider the supply chain that results in a restaurant pizza. The restaurant has to procure all the ingredients—from flour to tomato sauce to cheese to pepperoni. Few restaurants buy directly from farmers; most work through one or more intermediaries. Regardless of how many links there are in the supply chain for a given ingredient, risk must be managed. The restaurant may prefer to minimize its risk by paying a bit of a premium to ingredient suppliers willing to promise reliable delivery of fresh ingredients, regardless of circumstances. Those suppliers, in turn, may have contracts with food processors, and the processors may contract with the firms that buy wheat, tomatoes, milk, and livestock directly from farmers.

Ultimately, some combination of participants in the food supply chain must bear the risk that bad weather will make a product unavailable or at least more expensive than planned. Suppose, for example, that bad weather in Canada and Australia drives up the price of wheat. Depending on the nature of the supply chain arrangements, the restaurant may or may not end up paying a higher price for wheat flour in the short run.

If the restaurant does pay more for flour, it will either see a smaller profit margin or have to raise the price of pizza enough to offset the increase in ingredient prices. If it does not pay more, it means someone else in the supply chain is absorbing a short-term loss. Maybe the flour processor agreed to supply flour at a fixed price, and managed its risk by using futures markets for wheat to ensure that its net cost of obtaining wheat would lock in a reasonable rate of return on flour production. In such a case, the loser in the transaction would be the person or firm that sold the futures contract for less than its eventual value. The seller might be a farmer, or it might be someone who speculates in commodity markets.

Over time, higher costs must eventually be passed along the supply chain—one link in the chain cannot keep losing money forever. Eventually, bad weather will have an effect on consumer food prices even if other parties in the food supply chain sometimes bear the cost in the short run.

Looking Ahead

Research may lead to new technologies that reduce the effect of weather on food production and prices. Still, it is hard to imagine a world where the weather has no impact on food prices. In fact, if global warming or natural variation in climate results in greater weather variability in the future, the variability in food prices may also increase.

If countries reduce trade barriers and the cost of moving food around the world, the effects of future weather-induced yield shocks will be more widely shared. Currently, trade restrictions mean that domestic market prices for food in some countries do not change much or at all when food prices change in other countries. If trade barriers are reduced, domestic market prices for food in different countries are likely to move together. As more producers and consumers respond to similar price signals, the overall variability of the prices of food traded in international markets should be reduced. A crop shortfall in one country can be offset by small adjustments in consumption in many countries, rather than large adjustments in just a few.

On the other hand, suppose new government trade barriers, a strong preference for local foods, or a sharp increase in fuel prices makes it difficult or impossible to trade food. With limited trade, food prices in one country would be less dependent on the weather in another country, but changes in local weather conditions could have much larger impacts on domestic food prices. A drought in one country would result in a very large increase in food prices in the domestic market, but would have little or no effect on food prices in other countries.

In the meantime, the weather is one important indicator of future food prices. Pay particular attention at the times and in the places that matter most to the world's food production—summer rainfall in Iowa is very important, winter temperatures in Siberia are not. Until we can develop perfect long-range weather forecasts, it will be impossible to develop perfect forecasts of food prices. Even if we understand and can forecast all the other factors affecting food prices, weather volatility means there will always be considerable uncertainty around food price projections.

Chapter 5

Money in the Pocket, Food on the Plate

Rich people don't starve and poor people don't eat caviar. The causes of hunger are complex, but to put it simply, hunger occurs when people cannot obtain the food they need. Many people produce at least some of the food they eat, but most people must buy some or all of the food they consume. When people don't have enough money in their pockets, they may not be able to put enough food on their plates.

Income affects how much people eat and what kinds of food they choose to buy. A hungry person who gets an increase in income is likely to buy more food. Someone who can already afford a basic diet may not buy much *more* food in response to an increase in income, but they may change the *types* of food they buy. Maybe they buy less rice and wheat flour and instead buy more fruits, vegetables, meats, dairy products, and processed foods. Higher income consumers may eat out more often or spend a little extra on organic foods or premium coffee.

Because incomes affect what we eat, incomes also affect food prices. When incomes rise, demand for many types of food increases, and demand for other types of food declines. In a very low-income country where people struggle just to satisfy basic nutritional needs, higher incomes may increase the demand for grains, vegetable oil, and other foods that dominate the diets of low-income people. In a middle-income country, higher incomes may cause an increase in the demand for meat and dairy products. When food demand increases, the result is an increase in food prices unless food supplies keep pace.

This brings us to another rule of thumb: *Food prices rise when incomes rise and fall when incomes fall.*

It should not be surprising that increases in income result in higher prices for "luxury" foods. It is less obvious why higher incomes raise food prices in general. After all, people can only eat so much. Once basic needs are satisfied, the total quantity of food a person consumes may not increase that much (or at all) when incomes increase. Certainly, you could find examples of specific food items that are in less demand when the economy is doing well than during a recession—think of generic macaroni sold at big box supermarkets, for example. However, higher incomes are likely to increase demand and prices for more types of food than are likely to experience price reductions.

Consider the case of basic staples like milled rice, wheat flour, or corn tortillas. When the world economy is growing and incomes are rising around the world, many middle- and high-income consumers may reduce their demand for these basic staples as they increase consumption of other, higher-valued foods. Per-capita rice consumption has actually declined as incomes have increased in many Asian countries in recent decades, for example. By itself, this would tend to put downward pressure on prices for rice and other cereals.

Still, this does not mean that a strong global economy will result in lower prices for basic cereals. First, many of the world's poor have not reached the point where more income causes them to buy more meat and less bread. They may increase their total food purchases when their incomes increase, and that may mean increased demand even for the most basic cereals.

Second, higher incomes are generally associated with increased demand for meat and dairy products. To produce these animal products, more cattle, chickens, and hogs are fed more grain and oilseed meal. This increase in the amount of grain fed to livestock and poultry may outweigh any reduction in direct human use of grain as a food. Thus, the net effect of higher incomes may be to increase global demand for grain and grain prices.

It takes several pounds of feed to make a pound of meat or cheese. Just how many pounds it takes depends on the animal product, how it is produced and how one does the accounting.[1] When people start consuming more animal products in their diets, it generally increases the total demand for grain and oilseeds, even if some people eat less rice, bread, and tortillas.

The 2005–2009 Experience

World economic growth was generally very strong from 2005 until the middle of 2008, and this contributed to rising demand for food in many countries and higher global food prices. China and India, for example, both had phenomenal rates of economic growth. According to the World Bank, GDP growth in China exceeded 10 percent per year in 2005 and 2006 and reached 13 percent in 2007. GDP growth in India was almost as fast, exceeding 9 percent per year from 2005 to 2007. For comparison, the U.S. economy grew at an average rate of 2.6 percent per year between 2005 and 2007.[2]

When two countries that together have more than a third of the world's population grow at such an incredible pace, it has impacts on markets for everything from food to petroleum to steel. Food demand growth in China and India was so strong between 2005 and mid-2008 that both countries increased consumption levels of a wide range of food items in the face of higher prices. Increased food demand in China, India, and other fast-growing countries put upward pressure on food prices around the world.

In China, rising incomes over the 2005-2008 period contributed to a 19 percent increase in chicken consumption and smaller increases for beef and pork (see Table 5.1). Demand for dairy products also increased rapidly, with consumption of fluid milk and whole milk powder both increasing by more than 20 percent in just three years.

Table 5.1   *Chinese Consumption of Agricultural Products, 2005 and 2008, Million Metric Tons*

	2005	2008	Absolute Change	Percentage Change
Pork	45.1	46.4	1.2	3%
Chicken	10.1	12.0	1.9	19%
Beef	5.6	6.1	0.4	8%
Sum of 3 meats	60.8	64.4	3.6	6%
Fluid milk	12.5	15.3	2.8	22%
Whole milk powder	1.0	1.2	0.2	24%
Corn	131.0	149.0	18.0	14%
Rice	130.3	127.5	-2.9	-2%
Wheat	102.0	106.0	4.0	4%
Sum of 3 grains	363.3	382.5	19.2	5%
Soybean meal	23.4	30.8	7.4	32%
Soybean oil	7.2	9.7	2.5	35%
Palm oil	4.4	5.2	0.9	20%
Sum of 2 oils	11.6	14.9	3.4	29%

Note: Meat, poultry, and dairy data are for calendar years 2005 and 2008. Grain, soybean meal, and vegetable oil data are for marketing years 2004/05 and 2007/08.

Source: USDA PSD Online data set, September 2009.

To feed growing livestock herds and poultry flocks, China rapidly increased its use of both corn and soybean meal. Corn use increased by 14 percent between the 2004/2005 and the 2007/2008 marketing years, while soybean meal consumption grew by an astounding 32 percent. Rice consumption, on the other hand, declined slightly, as some consumers shifted to other foods. Vegetable oil consumption also increased sharply, with soybean oil use increasing by 35 percent and palm oil consumption up 20 percent. Many of these increases in food consumption would be noteworthy in any circumstances, but they are particularly remarkable considering how rapidly world food prices rose between 2005 and mid-2008.

The story in India is a little different, but also very important. For cultural and economic reasons, India has very low levels of meat consumption, so one might not expect animal agriculture to play a major role in food demand growth. Still, both chicken and beef consumption grew quickly in India between 2005 and 2008 (see Table 5.2). Although many Indians do not eat meat, consumption of dairy products is near the world average and is growing very rapidly. Fluid milk consumption

Table 5.2 *Indian Consumption of Agricultural Products, 2005 and 2008, Million Metric Tons*

	2005	2008	Absolute Change	Percentage Change
Chicken	1.9	2.5	0.6	31%
Beef	1.6	1.8	0.2	13%
Sum of 2 meats	3.5	4.3	0.8	23%
Fluid milk	36.6	43.9	7.3	20%
Butter and ghee	2.7	3.7	0.9	34%
Corn	13.9	14.2	0.3	2%
Rice	80.9	90.5	9.6	12%
Wheat	72.8	76.3	3.5	5%
Sum of 3 grains	167.6	181.0	13.4	8%
Soybean meal	1.4	2.1	0.6	44%
Soybean oil	2.6	2.3	-0.3	-12%
Palm oil	3.4	4.6	1.2	35%
Sum of 2 oils	6.0	6.9	0.9	15%

Note: Meat, poultry, and dairy data are for calendar years 2005 and 2008. Grain, soybean meal, and vegetable oil data are for marketing years 2004/05 and 2007/08.

Source: USDA PSD Online data set, September 2009.

increased by 20 percent in just three years, and consumption of butter and ghee (a type of clarified butter) rose by 34 percent.

In India, most of the recent growth in grain demand can be attributed to increased human consumption rather than growth in livestock feed demand. Between 2004/2005 and 2007/2008, estimated rice consumption in India grew by 12 percent. Recall that rice consumption in China fell over the same period. Average income levels in India are lower than in China, so Indian consumers are more likely than Chinese consumers to increase their purchases of basic staple grains when their incomes increase.

As in China, Indian consumption of vegetable oil also increased sharply, as the large increase in palm oil consumption far outweighed a small reduction in soybean oil use. Both soybean oil and palm oil prices increased by about 150 percent between 2004/2005 and 2007/2008.[3] Once again, the willingness to consume more of a product at a higher price is a sign of just how strong the growth in demand was.

China and India are not the only countries that experienced rapid income growth over the 2005-2008 period, and they are not the only countries that saw significant increases in food demand. Mexico, for example, significantly increased consumption of poultry and milk, and imported more corn to be used as feed for livestock and poultry. The economy of Bangladesh grew by more than 6 percent per year from 2005 to 2007, and rice consumption increased by 14 percent between 2004/05 and 2007/08.[4]

After years of solid growth, the economies of the United States, Europe, and Japan entered a severe recession in the final months of 2008. GDP fell at an alarming rate in most high-income countries, and economic growth at least slowed in almost every country around the world. Credit markets tightened, major firms collapsed or survived only with government aid, unemployment rose, and consumer confidence dropped to extremely low levels. International prices for food, oil, and a wide range of other commonly traded goods fell sharply as economic activity slowed and trade contracted.

The world economic crisis had severe effects on world food markets. Reduced demand, especially for meats, dairy products, and other high-value foods, resulted in lower prices. The weaker global economy reduced the demand for petroleum, resulting in lower crude oil prices. As discussed in previous chapters, this reduces the cost of producing and transporting food and weakens demand for biofuels. With less demand for animal products and biofuels, there is less demand for the grain and oilseeds used to feed livestock or produce ethanol and biodiesel.

Market developments in the final months of 2008 are consistent with this story for a wide range of food products. Milk and dairy product prices declined sharply, for example, as demand weakened in response to the global economic crisis. In the United States, the average price paid to farmers for milk fell by 40 percent between July 2008 and February 2009.[5] The price decline did not result from an increase in domestic production, as USDA estimated that 2009 U.S. milk production would fall below the 2008 level.[6] Instead, it was the collapse of U.S. dairy product exports, which meant that more of the nation's milk production had to be absorbed in a domestic U.S. market hit hard by the recession. Milk and dairy product prices also declined in Europe and most other milk-producing countries.

U.S. agricultural product exports increased from $63 billion in fiscal year 2005 to $115 billion in fiscal year 2008.[7] After running well above the levels of the previous year for most of 2008, the pace of U.S. agricultural exports slowed dramatically in the final months of 2008 (see Figure 5.1). By March 2009, the value of U.S. agricultural exports was down by 24 percent from the same month in 2008. While lower income growth in other countries contributed to the decline in U.S. agricultural exports, lower income growth at home also reduced the demand for agricultural imports. In the first months of 2009, the value of U.S. agricultural imports was also running below year-ago levels.[8] This pattern of reduced trade in both directions is common when recessions reduce global demand.

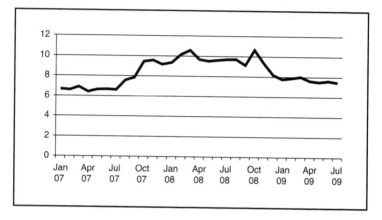

Figure 5.1 *U.S. agricultural exports, billion dollars*

Source: The USDA's Economic Research Service, "Foreign Agricultural Trade of the United States," September 2009.

U.S. retail food price inflation also slowed sharply in the final months of 2008. Seasonally adjusted monthly food price inflation peaked at 0.9 percent in July 2008, a rate that would have resulted in double-digit annual food price inflation had it persisted for an entire year. By December 2008, monthly food price inflation was down to less than 0.1 percent, and preliminary estimates indicate that U.S. consumer food prices actually fell slightly in the early months of 2009.[9] A weaker global economy contributed to a sharp reduction in prices paid to farmers for many of the products they sell and a slight decline in consumer food prices. The recession may have devastated many household budgets, but at least it helped reduce the cost of a trip to the supermarket.

Why the Story Is a Little More Complicated

Economic growth and income levels do have very real and important impacts on food demand and prices. Still, the full story is not as neat and tidy as the discussion so far would suggest.

The China Story

History did not begin in 2005 and economic growth in China, India, and other countries is not a brand new phenomenon. The World Bank estimates that the Chinese economy grew at an average annual rate of almost 10 percent between 1990 and 2005, only slightly less than the average growth rate between 2005 and 2007.[10] That means the Chinese economy was more than four times as large in 2005 as it was in 1990. Yet if one looks at a graph of world grain prices, there was no distinct trend between 1990 and 2005. Why would economic growth in China suddenly make world food prices increase rapidly from 2005 to 2008 when it did not have that effect in earlier years?

This is not a new question. In 1995, Lester Brown's book *Who Will Feed China? Wake-Up Call for a Small Planet* made the argument that Chinese food consumption would diversify and grow in response to rising incomes. Furthermore, Brown warned that resource constraints would limit Chinese food production and that the resulting increases in Chinese food imports soon would result in rapid and unsustainable increases in world food prices.[11] The book appeared prophetic when a sudden sharp increase in Chinese grain imports contributed to a large increase in world grain prices in 1995 and 1996. Just a few years later, however, China was again largely self-sufficient in grain production and world grain prices fell back to pre-boom levels.

Brown and others were not wrong to suggest that rising incomes would result in changes in Chinese diets. Chinese GDP and meat consumption have been increasing for many years. Current USDA estimates indicate that total Chinese consumption of beef, pork, and chicken now far exceeds consumption of the same meats in the United States (see Figure 5.2). In per-capita terms, Chinese meat consumption levels remain much lower than in the United States or other high-income countries, but the gap has narrowed considerably in recent years. In 2008, for example, Chinese meat consumption per capita was about 43 percent of the U.S. level, based on USDA estimates. Total meat consumption in China exceeds that in the United States because China's population is so much greater (1.33 billion in China vs. 305 million in the United States in 2008).[12]

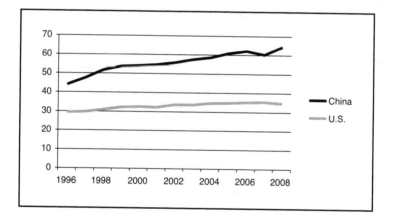

Figure 5.2 *Consumption of beef, pork, and chicken, million metric tons*

Source: Author calculations based on the USDA's data set, "Production, Supply, and Distribution Online," September 2009.

If meat consumption in China has been growing for some time, then it is much more difficult to make the argument that sudden shifts in demand caused by higher Chinese incomes were a major cause of rising world food prices between 2005 and 2008. Chinese demand for grain, oilseed meals, and vegetable oils also has been increasing for quite some time. This rising demand means that it takes increasing supplies in China and other countries to contain world food prices, but it is hard to argue that Chinese economic growth added something fundamentally new to the world food price equation after 2005.

The key is how growth in Chinese demand affects world food markets. If China is able to increase its domestic production fast enough to keep up with rising food demand, there may be little impact on the rest of the world. Contrary to the expectations of Brown and others, China has so far been able to rapidly increase its production of grain and meat to largely keep pace with rising domestic food demand. In recent years, China has actually exported more corn, wheat, and rice than it imports, and trade in beef and pork continues to be very small relative to Chinese consumption levels. For several years, China was able to sustain grain exports only by sharply drawing down large grain inventories, but even this practice appears to have ended in recent years. China did contribute to higher world grain prices by reducing its corn exports in 2007/2008, but otherwise rapid economic growth in China had little direct effect on world grain markets.

There is one glaring and critical exception to the general rule that Chinese food production has been able to keep pace with consumption. Many years ago, China gave up any pretense of being self-sufficient in oilseed production. The country is easily the world's largest importer of soybeans, and those imports continued to grow at a frantic pace between 2005 and 2008, in spite of much higher prices in world oilseed markets. China crushes imported soybeans to make soybean oil for people to use in food preparation, and soybean meal to feed livestock, poultry, and fish.

What will happen in the future to Chinese food consumption and trade is of obvious importance to the world food system. Baseline projections prepared by the Food and Agricultural Policy Research

Institute in early 2009 suggest China may eventually become a net importer of corn and that growth in Chinese oilseed consumption and imports will continue to put upward pressure on world markets. Projected Chinese consumption of grains, meats, and dairy products all grow in response to assumed future Chinese economic growth, and production growth generally keeps pace with rising consumption. As a result, trade in those products remains very small relative to production and consumption; except for oilseeds, China does not dominate world food trade.[13]

One lesson from past experience is that all projections of Chinese food markets prove to be wrong. Even explaining the past can be hazardous, because data are often unreliable and subject to very large revisions. If something causes even a modest change in the supply-demand balance in China, the implications for world markets and food prices could be very large. If Chinese meat consumption continues to grow at the recent pace but grain production slows, for example, China could become a large food importer, and this would put severe upward pressure on world food prices.

China: A Brief Diversion

Attentive readers may have noticed something odd about Figure 5.2. Why did Chinese meat consumption decline temporarily in 2007? As described at greater length in Chapter 8, "Stuff Happens," part of the story is tied to a hog disease (porcine reproductive and respiratory syndrome, better known as blue ear disease) that contributed a significant decline in Chinese pork production. The reduction in Chinese pork supplies caused a dramatic increase in pork prices in China— between June 2006 and April 2008, retail pork prices in China increased by 143 percent.[14] China is normally self-sufficient in pork production, but the run-up in Chinese prices resulted in pork imports into China.

Not only did this hog disease outbreak have a large impact on Chinese pork markets, but it also affected international markets for pork, grains, and oilseed meals. It forced Chinese government officials to pay close attention to the agricultural sector, as the temporary sharp increase in domestic pork prices significantly increased the cost of living. This increased attention to questions of food security could drive policy decisions for years to come.

China and India in Perspective

Rising incomes in China, India, and other countries did make an important contribution to the increase in world food demand and prices between 2005 and 2008, but it is important to keep that role in perspective. Between the 2004/2005 and 2007/2008 marketing years, total world consumption of corn, wheat, and rice increased by about 6 percent. In China and India combined, total consumption of those three grains also increased by about 6 percent. In other words, grain consumption in India and China only grew at about the same pace as grain consumption in the world as a whole.

Considering the sharp increase in grain prices between 2005 and the early months of 2008, any increase in grain consumption suggests demand for grain must have been very strong, and rising incomes in China and India are certainly part of the story. Still, grain consumption also grew in other countries where economic growth was much slower than in China and India. Much of that growth in grain consumption occurred in the United States.

Growth in U.S. ethanol use of grain accounted for more of the increase in world grain consumption than did economic growth in China and India.[15] In the case of oilseeds, on the other hand, growth in Chinese and Indian demand was a dominant factor. Income-driven growth in food demand in China, India, and other countries was an important part of the food price story, but biofuels and other forces also played a major role in increasing food demand and prices.

Income and Food Consumption in High-Income Countries

In the United States, the total amount of food consumed does not change very much when incomes rise or fall. Many people find it difficult to afford an adequate and nutritious diet, but few North Americans suffer from a shortage of calories. A third of U.S. adults are classified as obese, and obesity affects all income groups.[16] When their incomes rise and fall, people are more likely to adjust what and where they eat more than how much they eat in total.

The link between economic growth and total consumption of meat, poultry, and dairy products is weaker in high-income countries than it is in lower-income countries. Preliminary estimates from USDA suggest that the worst recession in decades will reduce per-capita meat consumption in the United States in 2009 by only about 2 percent.[17] However, people adjust the types of meat they buy as incomes change. For example, a recession may lead some people to buy less steak and more hamburger. Very tentative support for this hypothesis is provided by looking at the evolution of retail prices of different types of beef as the recession worsened. Between August 2008 and February 2009, the average price of ground beef increased slightly, from $2.37 per pound to $2.44 per pound, while the average retail price of boneless sirloin steak declined from $6.40 per pound to $5.68 per pound over the same period.[18]

Changes in income may also affect where people buy food. In a recession, people may be more likely to eat at home than to eat out. When they do eat out, they may be more likely to stop at a fast food place than an upscale restaurant. When they buy groceries, they may be more likely to go to stores better known for low prices than premium foods. This push to go back to basics may affect a wide range of consumer purchases, not just of food. Of course, there will always be exceptions. For example, some people may buy more "comfort foods" when they are worried about their jobs and how they are going to pay the bills.

The 2008–2009 recession reduced U.S. consumer spending on food and most other goods and services. Real consumer spending on food fell in the third and fourth quarters of 2008 as the recession deepened. Yet the data also show that consumer spending on food was much more stable than spending on cars and other durable goods. According to preliminary data from the U.S. Department of Commerce,[19] real consumer spending on food and beverages fell by 3 percent between the second and fourth quarters of 2008, while spending on motor vehicles fell by 15 percent over the same period.

Managing the Food Supply Chain When Consumer Demand Shifts

Just as a weather-induced change in crop supplies has effects up and down the food supply chain, shifts in demand can also affect everyone involved in the process of getting food from the farmer to the consumer. When rapid economic growth causes an increase in consumer demand for beef, for example, suppliers need to find a way to provide what consumers want. In the short run, there is only so much beef in the world, and the only way to satisfy increased demand from one group of consumers is to divert beef supplies that would have gone to other consumers, and that usually means higher prices.

Over time, these price signals will be passed back from restaurants and grocers to wholesalers, beef processors, and livestock producers. Beef processors will compete for available supplies of live cattle, driving up prices paid for cattle leaving the feedlots where they are fattened. These higher prices for fed cattle, in turn, will make feedlot owners willing to pay more for the younger feeder cattle they buy from ranchers. Higher prices for feeder cattle provide an incentive to ranchers to increase the number of calves they raise.

To get a calf requires a cow and time. On any day there are only so many cows, and the only way for the world as a whole to get more cows is to send fewer cows and heifers (young female cattle) to slaughter. Both of these choices can actually reduce beef supplies in the short run. From the time a cow is bred to the time a calf is born is nine months, and even after a calf is born, it takes more than a year before that calf will reach slaughter weight. Thus it takes a long time from a shift in beef demand to the time the supply chain can fully respond.

For some other types of food, the supply chain can respond much more rapidly to a change in consumer demand. Poultry production, for example, can be increased relatively quickly once a signal is given. In almost no cases, however, can supplies adjust instantaneously to a shift in demand. When the 2008 recession hit hard and with little warning, it disrupted food supply chains around the world. Some participants in the food system were smart or lucky enough to manage those risks successfully; others were caught unprepared and unprotected, and some of them are now out of business.

To be successful, firms in the food industry must find ways to manage both supply and demand risk. Different firms in different parts of the industry have pursued different strategies. Some choose to own or otherwise control various links in the supply chain. For example, major firms in the poultry industry contract chicken production with individual growers, own processing plants, and market their own products. Others diversify their holdings or use other risk management tools to ensure that bad luck or a bad decision will not drive them into bankruptcy.

Making Sense of It All

Some major conclusions:

Rising incomes increase consumption of a wide range of foods. Rising incomes are especially likely to increase consumption of meat, poultry, and dairy products, particularly in countries where much of the population is neither desperately poor nor excessively rich.

When meat and dairy consumption increases, more grains and oilseed meals are used to feed the world's livestock and poultry. This indirect effect of higher incomes on grain and oilseed demand may in some cases be larger than the direct effect of higher incomes on consumption of bread, rice, tortillas, and other staple foods.

Changes in consumption are not a perfect indicator of the effects of income on food prices. Even modest increases in consumption in the face of large increases in food prices suggest that the underlying demand for food is very strong. Were it not for income growth, one would expect a large increase in food prices to result in reduced food consumption.

When a recession reduces incomes, the result is likely to be lower food prices. All the factors that make food prices increase when incomes rise are likely to drive down food prices when incomes fall. The global recession was an important factor driving down world food prices in the final months of 2008.

Two final points are in order. First, consider what happens when income growth is uneven across countries or segments of the population. People with rising incomes can afford more and higher-valued foods, and this will tend to result in higher food prices for everyone. If some vulnerable populations are forced to pay higher prices for food but do not share in the income growth, the result may be an increase in hunger. A broad-based increase in income levels is almost certain to reduce hunger, but if economic growth leaves a lot of people behind, the net impact on hunger is not as clear. That is one reason why decades of world income growth still leaves about a billion people hungry.

Second, prices depend on both supply and demand. Rising incomes do not have to mean higher food prices if food production growth is fast enough. Likewise, a drought may not result in higher food prices if a global recession is sharply reducing food consumption. From 2005 until the middle of 2008, both supply and demand factors were pushing food prices higher, and in the final months of 2008, both supply and demand factors were pushing food prices lower.

Chapter 6

Food Appreciation and Dollar Depreciation

Currency exchange rates affect the prices of everything from cars to corn. When the U.S. dollar gets stronger against other currencies, it reduces the dollar price of items the United States imports from other countries. For goods the United States exports, a stronger dollar makes U.S. products more expensive in terms of foreign currency.

Most types of food are traded in international markets, so currency exchange rates are an important factor affecting food prices. When the dollar weakens or strengthens against other currencies, food prices are likely to respond. Thus, the next rule of thumb: *Food prices measured in dollars increase when the dollar weakens against other currencies and decrease when the dollar strengthens.*

Currency exchange rates are one reason why there is no such thing as *the* world price of food. Sure, people point to various indicators when they talk about world food prices, and some of these indicators are very useful. This book is full of useful but imperfect indicators of world food prices. None of them really provide a truly correct and global picture of what farmers get for the food they sell or consumers pay for the food they buy.

Consider what might seem to be a very simple question: How much did the price of corn change between December 2006 and December 2008? It might not seem like a trick question, but there are actually many equally correct answers. The problem is that on any given day, there are many different prices for corn. Farmers in Iowa get one price for the corn they sell and poultry producers in North Carolina pay a different price for the corn they buy. Farmers in isolated villages in Latin America or Africa get very different prices for the corn they grow, and corn consumers in Mexico City or Nairobi pay very different prices for the corn they buy.

So let's try to be even more specific. The United States is the world's largest exporter of corn and most U.S. corn exports are put on ocean-going ships in the Gulf of Mexico, so the price of number 2 yellow corn (the benchmark grade) in gulf ports is often referred to as the "world price" of corn. How much did this particular corn price change between December 2006 and December 2008? Looking at USDA data, the December 2006 price averaged $160.62 per metric ton and the price in December 2008 averaged $158.26 per metric ton.[1] Corn prices had a wild ride over that two-year period, but ended up at about the same place they started.

Japan and Mexico are the two largest export markets for U.S. corn. Suppose someone in Japan bought U.S. corn in December 2006, and paid with Japanese yen. In December 2006, a dollar sold for 117.13 yen,[2] so a metric ton of corn loaded on a ship in the U.S. gulf was worth 18,814 yen ($160.62 per ton, multiplied by 117.13 yen per dollar). Two years later, a dollar sold for just 91.32 yen. In other words, the yen had strengthened considerably against the dollar, or from the U.S. perspective, the dollar had weakened considerably against the yen. In December 2008, a metric ton of corn loaded on a ship in the U.S. gulf was worth just 14,453 yen ($158.26 per ton, multiplied by 91.32 yen per dollar). While the price of corn measured in dollars only fell by 1 percent between December 2006 and December 2008, the same price measured in yen fell by 23 percent.

Now consider a Mexican buyer of U.S. corn. In December 2006, a dollar sold for 10.87 pesos, so a metric ton of corn in the U.S. gulf was worth 1,745 pesos ($160.62 per ton, multiplied by 10.87 pesos per dollar). In December 2008, a dollar sold for 13.37 pesos, so a metric ton of corn in the U.S. gulf was worth 2,116 pesos ($158.26 per ton multiplied by 13.37 pesos per dollar). The weakening of the peso relative to the dollar (or, depending on your perspective, the strengthening of the dollar relative to the peso) meant that the U.S. corn price rose by 21 percent in peso terms between December 2006 and the same month two years later.

To summarize: Between December 2006 and December 2008, the world price of corn

- Stayed about the same when measured in dollars
- Fell by 23 percent when measured in yen
- Rose by 21 percent when measured in pesos

Because the price measured in yen fell, livestock producers and other purchasers of U.S. corn in Japan would have had an incentive to buy more U.S. corn than they would have if the dollar had not weakened against the yen. In Mexico, the opposite is true. Because the price measured in pesos increased, Mexican users of U.S. corn would have had an incentive to use less U.S. corn than if the dollar had not strengthened against the peso.

Changes in exchange rates will not always have the expected effects on food trade patterns because of all the other forces that affect food supply and demand around the world. In reality, for example, estimated Japanese corn imports were about the same during the 2008/2009 marketing year as during the 2006/2007 year. However, preliminary estimates do show a significant decline in Mexican corn imports in 2008/2009,[3] and the strengthening of the dollar against the peso is at least one contributing factor.

If you are a U.S. tourist traveling abroad, a stronger dollar is a good thing, as it makes foreign hotels, meals, and gift items cheaper in dollar terms. However, if you are someone trying to sell U.S. farm products overseas, a stronger dollar is not such a good thing, as it makes U.S. goods more expensive when purchased with foreign currency. When foreign buyers face higher prices in their domestic currency, they are not likely to buy as much. When foreign competitors face higher prices in their domestic currency, they are likely to produce and export more. The resulting reduction in U.S. exports results in lower prices measured in dollars, unless some other larger factor offsets the effect of a stronger dollar. The reverse, of course, is true when the dollar weakens.

Exchange rates have varied a lot in recent years, and as shown by the Mexican and Japanese examples, the dollar may be strengthening against some currencies at the same time it is weakening against others. That makes it hard to sort out the net effect of exchange rate movements on food prices. In a sense, this is somewhat like the effect of weather. Good weather results in increased food production in one country at the same time that poor weather reduces food production in another country. When this happens, the net effect of the world's weather on food prices is small and hard to measure. When the dollar weakens against some currencies and strengthens against others, the net effect of these exchange rate movements on prices measured in dollars may also be small and hard to measure.

At other times, however, bad weather in some major producing countries is not offset by good weather elsewhere, reducing global food production and raising food prices. Likewise, sometimes the value of the dollar weakens against most major currencies at the same time. When that happens, food becomes more expensive when measured in dollar terms, even at the same time it gets cheaper when measured in the currencies of other countries.

The 2005–2009 Experience

Between 2005 and the middle of 2008, the dollar weakened against a number of major foreign currencies. While this held down the rate of food price increases in other countries, it made food prices increase even more rapidly when measured in dollars. In the last half of 2008, the dollar strengthened against most major currencies. The result was a sharper decline in food prices as measured in dollar terms than when measured in terms of other currencies. The dollar weakened again in the first half of 2009, providing support for food prices measured in dollars.

The evolution of soybean prices and exchange rates between 2005 and 2009 is consistent with this story. The dollar cost of soybeans to an Illinois processor increased by 168 percent between September of 2005 and July 2008 (see Figure 6.1). As with grains and many other food products, soybean prices then fell sharply in the final months of 2008, declining by 43 percent between July and December 2008. Soybean prices then rebounded in early 2009.

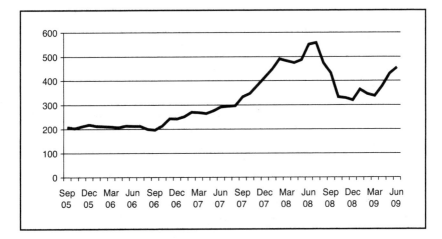

Figure 6.1 *U.S. processor price for soybeans, dollars per metric ton*

Source: Monthly price data from the USDA's Economic Research Service and Agricultural Marketing Service.

The United States is the world's largest producer of soybeans, and the Illinois processor price is often used as an indicator of world market conditions. The European Union is a major importer of soybeans and soybean products, and Brazil is a major exporter competing with the United States in world markets. Exchange rates between the dollar and the currencies of the European Union and Brazil will have a significant impact on world soybean market prices.

Between September 2005 and July 2008, the dollar declined in value relative to the euro by 22 percent (see Figure 6.2). Over that same period, the dollar declined in value relative to the Brazilian real by 31 percent (see Figure 6.3). In the final months of 2008, the dollar strengthened against both currencies. Between July and December 2008, the dollar rose in value by 16 percent against the euro and by 50 percent against the real. Comparing Figures 6.1, 6.2, and 6.3, the movements in U.S. soybean prices and in exchange rates appear to mirror one another.

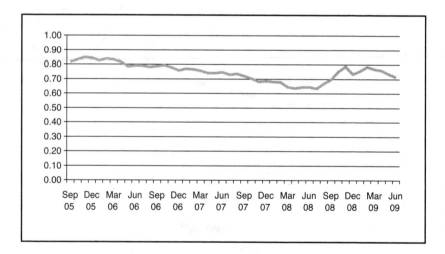

Figure 6.2   *Exchange rate, euro per dollar*

Source: International Financial Statistics data, International Monetary Fund

When the dollar declined in value against the euro, it helped hold down the price of soybeans to European processors. In turn, that

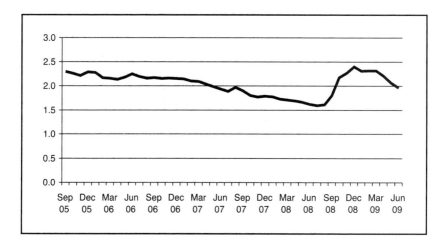

Figure 6.3 *Exchange rate, Brazilian reals per dollar*

Source: International Financial Statistics data, International Monetary Fund

helped hold down the price of soybean meal fed to European hogs, chickens and cows and the price of soybean oil used in everything from cooking oil to a wide range of processed foods. That helped support European demand for imported soybeans, which in turn supported the dollar price of soybeans in the United States.

Exchange rate changes also affect competing exporters. When the dollar declined in value against the Brazilian currency, it meant that any given U.S. dollar price for soybeans translated into a lower price for soybeans in Brazil. Lower prices for soybeans in Brazil, in turn, reduce incentives to Brazilian farmers to bring new lands into soybean production and encourage more domestic consumption of Brazilian soybeans. As a result, Brazil did not expand its soybean exports as rapidly as it would have were it not for the decline in the value of the dollar. Less competition from Brazil supported the dollar price of U.S. soybeans.

The strengthening of the dollar in the final months of 2008, of course, had just the opposite effects. It supported the local price of soybeans in the European Union, Brazil, and other countries. That meant that other countries consumed fewer soybeans than they would have otherwise, and competing southern hemisphere farmers planted more land to soybeans in late 2008 than they otherwise might have. With less import demand and more competing supplies, the dollar price of soybeans was pushed downward. Another exchange rate reversal in early 2009 again meant that a weaker dollar was supporting soybean prices measured in dollars.

The same holds for many other food products. Between 2005 and mid-2008, the weakening dollar made U.S. grains, oilseeds, meats, dairy products, fruits, and vegetables more affordable to consumers in other countries. This helped to push up prices for those foods measured in dollars. In the final months of 2008, the strengthening dollar made U.S. food products less affordable to consumers in other countries. This pushed down the price of food measured in dollars.

Why the Story Is a Little More Complicated

Exchange rates were an important factor in food markets between 2005 and 2009, but a more careful review of the evidence makes it clear that they can only explain a fraction of the observed changes in food prices.

Look Again

Figures 6.1 through 6.3 show that soybean prices and exchange rates moved in the expected directions relative to each other between 2005 and 2008. A weaker dollar coincided with rising soybean prices from 2005 until the middle of 2008, and a stronger dollar coincided with falling soybean prices in the final months of 2008.

A more careful examination of the figures raises some important questions. For example, if the dollar declined in value by 22 percent relative to the euro between September 2005 and July 2008, why did the price of soybeans increase by 168 percent? Likewise, how can a 16 percent rise in the value of the dollar against the euro in the final months of 2008 explain a 43 percent reduction in soybean prices? You might think the change in dollar prices should have been no greater than the change in exchange rates.

As Figure 6.4 shows, soybean prices increased between September 2005 and July 2008, regardless of the currency one uses to make the comparison. Yes, the increase was less in terms of euro or Brazilian reals than it was in terms of dollars, but soybean prices increased in terms of all three currencies. Likewise, soybean prices fell significantly in the final months of 2008 when measured in either dollars or euro. The sharp increase in the value of the dollar relative to the Brazilian currency in late 2008 meant that the decline in soybean prices measured in Brazilian reals was relatively modest.

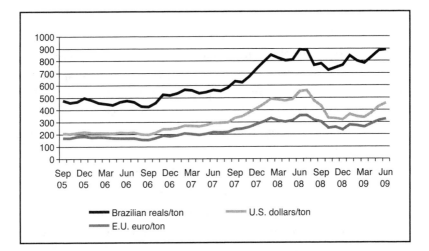

Figure 6.4 *U.S. soybean processor prices, currency per metric ton*

Source: Author calculations based on USDA, and IMF data.

The rebound in U.S. soybean prices and the renewed depreciation of the dollar in early 2009 pushed June 2009 soybean prices measured in Brazilian reals back up to the record levels of June 2008.

The simple exchange rate story can only explain a fraction of the changes in soybean prices between 2005 and 2009. Previous chapters have made it clear that many other factors contributed to the observed swings in food prices, so this result should not be a surprise. However, it is also possible that exchange rates have effects on food prices that go beyond those described so far.

Other Links between Exchange Rates and Food Prices

In a July 2008 report,[4] three Purdue University economists identified factors behind the rise in food prices in 2007 and 2008. The authors argued that some analysts had underestimated the role played by exchange rates. For example, they point out relationships between exchange rates and petroleum prices. A weaker dollar tends to go along with higher dollar prices for petroleum and vice versa. Many of the same reasons that exchange rates affect food markets also cause exchange rates to affect oil markets. For example, a weak dollar reduces foreign currency prices for oil, encouraging increased consumption in other countries. Increased global oil consumption, in turn, puts upward pressure on oil prices measured in dollars. Higher petroleum prices have major impacts on food prices, both because they affect the cost of producing food and because of their effects on biofuel markets.

Investors and speculators concerned about inflation can create another linkage between exchange rates and food prices. Because a weaker dollar drives up the cost of imported goods, investors worry more about inflation when the value of the dollar is falling. When investors fear inflation, they try to identify investment vehicles that will increase in value when prices are rising. Prices of commodities like oil, steel, grains, and oilseeds are more volatile than the average price of all goods and services in the economy. So investors and traders bet that commodity prices will rise faster than other prices in the general economy when inflation increases. If enough investors buy commodities futures at the same time, a rise in commodity prices becomes a self-fulfilling prophecy.

The relationship between food prices and exchange rates does not only work in one direction. For the United States, the value of food product trade is a relatively modest share of the overall trade balance, so it is unlikely that a change in food prices has much effect on exchange rates. The story may be different for countries more dependent on food exports and imports. For example, agricultural products account for a substantial share of Brazil's foreign trade. When food prices increase as much as they did between 2005 and mid-2008, the value of Brazilian exports increases sharply. A more positive trade balance, in turn, tends to result in a stronger currency. Thus, the movements in food prices help explain changes in exchange rates, just as exchange rate movements help explain changes in food prices.

Stronger, Weaker, and Broken Links

The linkage between food prices and exchange rates is only direct and clear when countries do not restrict food trade or fix food prices. If isolationist trade policies or high transportation costs cut local food markets off from the rest of the world, neither exchange rates nor food prices in other countries will have any direct effect on local food prices. Likewise, if governments directly manage food prices by using trade only to maintain a targeted level of food prices, exchange rates may have little or no impact on domestic food prices.

A change in the exchange rate between the dollar and the euro has important effects on food prices both in Europe and in the United

States. The European Union and United States are major food trading partners, so exchange rate movements affect food prices in both Europe and the United States. However, there are also many European food markets that are insulated from world market conditions by a complex set of trade and domestic policies. For those particular food products, exchange rates may have little direct effect on food prices.

In contrast, suppose the currency of a small country like Singapore appreciates relative to the U.S. dollar. Even if Singapore does not restrict food trade in any way, it is unlikely that the decrease in the value of the U.S. dollar against the country's currency will have any meaningful effect on food prices measured in U.S. dollars. U.S. food products will be more affordable in Singapore and that will drive down food prices in Singapore. However, even if this results in an increase in food imports by Singapore, the effects on global markets are likely to be quite small.

Exchange rates are likely to have a bigger impact on the price of traded farm commodities than on the price of a restaurant meal. Most of the cost of a restaurant meal is tied to labor costs, property rental, and other expenses not directly related to the price of traded goods and services. As a result, any effect of exchange rates on restaurant menu prices is likely to be muted. When the value of the dollar goes up, the cost of imported wine may come down, but the cook, waiter, and landlord still need to be paid.

Just as the food supply chain has to manage risk caused by uncertain crop yields and swings in the general economy, it also has to manage exchange rate risk. Firms can use futures markets and a wide range of other tools to smooth out the effects of short-term swings in exchange rates and in all the other factors that affect food prices.

One Factor among Many

Exchange rates are important, but they only explain a fraction of the movements in food prices between 2005 and 2009. In a remarkable coincidence, a wide variety of factors all pushed food prices higher between 2005 and the middle of 2008. Most of those same factors, including exchange rates, reversed course in the final months of 2008, and this contributed to a significant reduction in food prices.

When the value of the dollar falls relative to another currency, it pushes up prices measured in dollars and pushes down prices measured in the other currency. This is true in the case of almost anything that is traded across borders, whether it is oil or orange juice. Even in cases where the exchange rate effects are large, there will always be other forces that push food prices higher and lower.

Chapter 7

Speculating on Speculation

Every day, traders buy and sell thousands of contracts promising future delivery of wheat, corn, rice, soybeans, cattle, hogs, milk, sugar, and a number of other food products. The prices of these futures contracts rise and fall because of the buy and sell decisions made by market participants. If everybody tries to sell at the same time, prices fall until buyers are found; if everybody tries to buy at the same time, prices rise until sellers show up.

When food prices shot up in 2007 and 2008, many people blamed market speculators. They argued that traders had pushed the prices of food, oil, and other commodities above levels justified by market fundamentals, resulting in a speculative bubble. When prices fell sharply in the final months of 2008, this was seen as a sign that the speculative bubble had burst. Even if speculation had a short-run effect on food markets, however, it is difficult for prices to remain too high or too low for too long, as indicated in another rule of thumb: *Market speculators can push prices higher or lower, but fundamentals eventually rule.*

Futures markets are used for many reasons. Some buyers and sellers are trying to manage risks and use the futures market to lock in a price for future purchases or sales. A farmer wants to fix a price at planting time for corn or wheat to be harvested several months later. Food processors want to set a price in advance for grain that they will turn into pasta or pastries. Livestock producers want to lock in a price for the feed they buy and for the cattle or hogs they sell.

Other traders are speculators hoping to make money by correctly guessing how prices will move. A trader who believes prices will rise can buy a futures contract when prices are low and try to sell it later at a higher price. Speculators may have no other business connection to the product they are trading, and generally have no intention of ever owning corn, wheat, or hogs.

Still others buy futures contracts as part of an investment strategy or as a hedge against inflation. The prices of food products may not move in the same way as stock prices, so some investors see the purchase of a futures contract as a way to diversify their portfolios. Investors concerned about inflation buy futures contracts assuming that food prices will rise when there is an increase in the general price level.

Futures markets are tied to cash markets. For many food products, someone holding a futures contract has a legal right to receipt of a fixed amount of a product at set locations on certain dates. When markets are working properly, this means that the price of a futures contract should be very close to the cash price on the contract expiration date. For example, in early December, the futures price of corn for December delivery on the Chicago Mercantile Exchange should be very close to the actual market price of corn at specified delivery locations in Illinois.[1]

Traders in futures markets can use whatever information they consider relevant in deciding whether to buy or sell contracts at a given price. Some focus on market fundamentals—factors affecting current and future supply and demand for the product. Someone trading corn futures will consider the weather, the state of the economy, exchange rates, the price of petroleum, and all the other factors that affect the supply and demand of corn.

Other traders focus less on these market fundamentals and rely on other techniques to predict how prices are likely to change. Some of these technical traders carefully examine charts of futures prices in recent days, weeks, or even years and try to discern patterns suggesting how prices are likely to evolve. Others use statistical techniques to predict price movements.

Those investing in commodities such as corn or petroleum as a way to balance a portfolio or as a hedge against inflation pay little attention to day-to-day developments in futures markets. Instead, they put their money in index funds that hold futures contracts for a range of commodities. Some of these investors might not even know what commodities are included in their index funds, just as many owners of mutual funds do not know what companies are included in their stock portfolios. As with the range of mutual funds, some commodity index funds are managed actively, with constant adjustments in the mix of investments, whereas others limit themselves to a stable combination of commodity contracts owned.

Market commentators regularly disagree about the cause of daily movements in futures prices. Did a sharp increase in prices result from some change in market fundamentals, or did technical traders discern a chart signal to buy? Was a decline due to a favorable weather forecast or profit taking? Often it is hard to understand why traders make the choices they make, perhaps because traders are making choices based on varied sets of information and different motivations.

On any given day, the price of a futures contract is whatever traders decide it should be. An important question is how much that price is likely to differ from what the price would be based solely on market fundamentals. Separating price movements due to unjustified speculation from those caused by an appropriate consideration of supply and demand fundamentals is not easy. There is a mechanism that imposes some degree of discipline on the market, making it unlikely that prices will remain too far divorced from market fundamentals for too long.

Suppose that the price of corn in futures and cash markets is too low relative to market fundamentals for an extended period of time. In response to lower corn prices, livestock feeders use more corn and less wheat or sorghum. Biofuel producers use more cheap corn to make ethanol at a profit. Farmers plant less corn and more soybeans and wheat. As use increases and production falls, eventually the amount of corn left in storage falls to critical levels. Sooner or later, market participants realize the world is in danger of running out of corn, and prices are bid up to ration available supplies and encourage more production.

Now suppose that the corn price is too high relative to market fundamentals for an extended period. Livestock feeders scramble to find other feeds to replace corn, and may even reduce animal numbers. Ethanol plants are unable to operate profitably and shut down. Farmers plant more corn and less soybeans and wheat. The increase in production and reduction in use means that corn stocks accumulate. As long as prices are rising, it can be profitable to store grain, but once prices stop rising, those owning the corn will begin to wonder why they are spending money to store grain that no one seems to want. When firms are no longer willing to hold grain in storage, prices have to fall until buyers are found.

To say a speculative bubble of higher-than-justified prices cannot last forever is not the same as saying it can never develop in the first place. Even trying to determine whether prices are the result of undue speculation or market fundamentals is often very difficult. With the benefit of 20-20 hindsight, it is tempting to conclude that prices were ridiculously high or low in the past, and that the only possible explanation is irrational speculative behavior. It is harder to spot a bubble while it is occurring.

The 2005–2009 Experience

Market fundamentals contributed to the rise in food prices between 2005 and early 2008 and to the fall in food prices in the final months of 2008. Unfavorable weather in major grain-producing countries, economic growth, a weakening U.S. dollar, growth in biofuel production, increasing oil prices, and policies restricting supplies on world markets all contributed to the 2005–2008 rise in food prices. Better weather, the world financial crisis, a stronger dollar, slower biofuel production growth, declining oil prices, and policy adjustments all contributed to the decline in food prices in the last part of 2008.

Many analysts would add speculation to the list of causes of higher food prices in 2007 and early 2008. They argue that the increase in food prices cannot be explained by market fundamentals alone and that there is plenty of evidence that undue speculative behavior played an important role. A lot of new players invested in futures markets for food products, and most of the new money was on the demand side of the market, pushing prices up.

Index fund investments in food commodity futures grew rapidly during the period when food prices were increasing. For example, one analyst estimated that the Chicago wheat futures contract holdings of "index speculators" were almost seven times larger in March 2008 than in January 2003, and that these speculators held 64 percent of outstanding wheat contracts in 2008.[2] The index fund share of outstanding contracts for other food products also grew rapidly, although it accounted for a smaller share of the total market for other food products than it did for wheat.

A U.S. Senate subcommittee report argues that the expanding role of index funds in the wheat market not only pushed up wheat futures prices in 2007 and 2008, but also disrupted the normal relationship between cash and futures markets.[3] With so much index fund money pushing wheat futures prices higher, the futures price became disconnected from cash market prices, the report argued. Instead of wheat market prices being essentially the same as futures prices when contracts expired, cash market prices were much lower than futures prices in 2007 and 2008, and the relationship between cash and futures prices was very volatile. This made it very difficult for people who wanted to use futures markets as a tool to reduce risk.

Not only did index funds put a lot of money into food product markets when prices were rising; they also took money out of the markets in the final months of 2008 when prices fell. In the case of corn, positions held by index funds declined from 462,674 on July 1, 2008 to 273,415 on December 30, 2008.[4] The same story held for wheat, soybeans, and several other food products.

Index funds are not the only source of speculative behavior affecting food prices. If traders disregarded market fundamentals and bought futures simply because prices had been rising and they thought or hoped the trend would continue, this could have contributed to development of a speculative bubble. When the bubble popped, these traders quickly abandoned their positions, causing a sudden decline in market prices.

Why the Story Is a Little More Complicated

Before concluding that speculation was a major factor in food market developments between 2005 and 2009, remember that correlation is not the same as causation. Just because index funds increased investments in food product markets between 2005 and 2008 and food prices rose over the same period does not mean that the investments caused the price increases. Some analysts argue that cause-and-effect is more likely to operate in the opposite direction—index funds put lots of money into futures markets for food products because prices were rising and it seemed like a good investment. Likewise, the reduction in index fund positions in late 2008 may reflect the conclusion that food markets were not such a good place to invest after all.

Economists who have used statistical analysis to look at these questions have come to opposite conclusions. Economists from the International Food Policy Research Institute conducted several tests, some of which provided support for the argument that speculative activity affected market prices.[5] In contrast, Scott Irwin of the University of Illinois, a prominent economist, found no evidence that speculation played an important role in market price developments.[6]

Speculation and Stocks of Grain

There is no simple way to evaluate the arguments about the role played by speculation in food markets. It is very difficult to separate any effects of speculation from all the other factors that determine food prices. A proper assessment would require sophisticated statistical tests and even those might not yield a definitive conclusion. For our purposes, it may be useful to look instead at a relatively simple indicator to see whether it suggests any unusual market behavior between 2005 and 2008.

The stocks-to-use ratio measures the amount left in storage at the end of the year relative to the amount used during the course of the year. If the stocks-to-use ratio is very low, it indicates that available supplies are limited relative to demand, and this usually results in high market prices. If the stocks-to-use ratio is high, it suggests that there is plenty available to satisfy demand, and the normal result is low prices.

The relationship between this simple indicator and food prices is consistent with all market factors. When bad weather results in reduced crop production, less grain is available and less will be left in storage at the end of the year, resulting in a low stocks-to-use ratio and high prices. When income growth or increased biofuel demand results in greater use of grain, the stocks-to-use ratio will fall and prices will increase. Good weather, slow economic growth, or low oil prices all result in changes in supply and demand that cause stocks-to-use ratios to increase and prices to fall.

If stocks-to-use ratios appear inconsistent with market prices, it is a flag that something unusual is going on. If market speculation is keeping prices unreasonably high, for example, the resulting reduction in use and increase in production should result in an abnormally high stocks-to-use ratio relative to the market price. Therefore, a sharp increase in prices at the same time stocks-to-use ratios are also increasing points to market speculation as one possible cause.

The evidence from recent years is far from clear (see Table 7.1). Consider the corn market. Between 2000 and 2004, the average U.S. stocks-to-use ratio was 15 percent and the stocks-to-use ratio for the world as a whole was 22 percent. The average U.S. export price for corn was $100 per metric ton. In 2005/2006, the U.S. stocks-to-use ratio was higher than the 2000-2004 average and the world stocks-to-use ratio was lower. Given this mixed picture, it makes sense that the U.S. export price for corn was about the same as it had been over the previous five years. In 2006/2007, rising ethanol use and other demand growth around the world contributed to a reduction in both the U.S. and world stocks-to-use ratios, and prices rose significantly. All of these results are entirely consistent with market fundamentals.

The data for the 2007/2008 marketing year, however, look a bit peculiar. Both the U.S. and the world stocks-to-use ratios increased slightly, yet the U.S. export price for corn increased sharply. In other

Table 7.1   *Stocks-to-Use Ratios and World Prices*

	U.S. Stocks-to-Use Ratio	World Stocks-to-Use Ratio	World Price
Corn			
2000-2004 average	15%	22%	$100
2005/2006	17%	18%	$106
2006/2007	12%	15%	$155
2007/2008	13%	17%	$218
Wheat			
2000-2004 average	29%	29%	$144
2005/2006	27%	24%	$168
2006/2007	22%	21%	$204
2007/2008	13%	20%	$340
Rice			
2000-2004 average	14%	27%	$215
2005/2006	18%	18%	$301
2006/2007	18%	18%	$320
2007/2008	13%	19%	$551
Soybeans			
2000-2004 average	7%	21%	$218
2005/2006	16%	25%	$209
2006/2007	19%	28%	$259
2007/2008	7%	23%	$453

Notes: Stocks-to-use ratios measure the amount in storage, before the next crop is harvested, divided by annual usage. The reported world prices are export prices in the U.S. Gulf of Mexico for corn and wheat, Thai export prices for rice, and Illinois processor prices for soybeans, all in dollars per metric ton.

Source: Author calculations based on USDA data available in September 2009.

words, the market price in 2007/2008 seems very high relative to the stocks-to-use ratios. By no means is this firm proof of unwarranted market speculation causing high prices, but it does suggest further investigation is appropriate.

Before examining the corn story in more detail, consider the results for other major crops. In the case of wheat, both U.S. and world stocks-to-use ratios declined every year from 2005/2006 to 2007/2008 and U.S. export prices rose each year. Although the 2007/2008 price increase seems large relative to a modest decline in the world stocks-to-use ratio, it does not seem so unusual given the very low U.S. stocks-to-use ratio. With little competition from other exporters suffering from weather-induced declines in production, importers drained the U.S. market of almost all available wheat supplies, driving up prices to record highs in the process.

The story for rice is confusing. Because the United States is a relatively small player in world rice markets, it is not surprising that there is little obvious relationship between U.S. stocks-to-use ratios and the Thai price used as an indicator of world rice market conditions. More puzzling is the sharp increase in rice prices in 2007/2008 at the same time the world stocks-to-use ratio increased.

One part of the explanation is the policy response of several countries concerned about high food prices. India, Vietnam, and several other rice exporting countries restricted rice exports to make more food available in domestic markets. The result was a year-over-year increase in rice stocks, in spite of very high prices in world markets. Still, this explanation is not completely satisfactory, because it raises the question of why food prices increased in the first place, causing the policy response. One possible explanation is that the rise in wheat prices may have had spillover effects on the rice market as well; this explanation seems fairly plausible in India, but less so in other countries.

The case of soybeans also poses a puzzle, but one that is more easily solved. In 2006/2007, both the U.S. and world stocks-to-use ratios rose, yet the U.S. export price for soybeans rose as well. This result was far out of the historical norm and appears to provide evidence that speculation caused prices to rise above fundamental levels. However, in 2007/2008, both the U.S. and world stocks-to-use ratios fell and soybean market prices rose sharply. People who bought soybeans in 2006/2007, stored them, and then sold them in late 2007 or early 2008 made a handsome profit.

This helps make the point that the stocks-to-use ratio is not a perfect indicator of what market prices should be. In early 2007, it was clear that farmers in the United States were going to plant a lot more corn and a lot less soybeans than they had a year earlier in response to strong demand and prices for corn. People who held soybeans in storage knew that soybean production was likely to decline in 2007, and with continued strong global demand, the result was likely to be high soybean prices during the 2007/2008 marketing year. Rationally, they held onto their soybeans so they could sell them later at a higher price. The unusual relationship between soybean stocks-to-use ratios and soybean prices in 2006/2007 shows that market participants were looking at more than just current supply and demand fundamentals; they were also considering what those fundamentals would look like in the future. This is one form of market speculation, but it has a fundamental basis.

This brings us back to the corn story for 2007/2008. In late 2007 and early 2008, oil prices were rising and global demand for corn was strong. Many reasonable people expected oil prices to remain high or go higher in the years ahead, and few anticipated that a world financial crisis would sharply reduce global economic growth. Although it seemed clear there would be enough grain to satisfy world demand in 2007/2008, many expressed concerns about whether the world would have adequate supplies in later years. As a result, people were willing to hold on to corn stocks in spite of very high prices, as they expected prices to go even higher in the future.

So did this "excessive speculation" cause unwarranted increases in market prices? With the benefit of hindsight, it is clear that corn prices did not have to be so high to ration available supplies in 2007/2008, and there was plenty of corn to go around in 2008/2009. If everyone had known at the time what was actually going to occur, prices would not have increased so much in the first few months of 2008, and then there would have been no need for them to fall so hard in the final months of 2008. However, it is a lot easier to look back and say market actors behaved stupidly than it is to identify a speculative bubble while it is occurring. What seems obvious now was not so obvious at the time.

Cherry Picking

People trying to prove or disprove that market speculation resulted in food prices out of line with market fundamentals are prone to pick the statistics that make their point. For example, although it is true that index fund investments in food markets increased between 2003 and 2008, much of the increase occurred before the major run-up in food prices. While index fund investments and grain prices both fell in late 2008, more recent data tells a different story. Index fund investment picked up again in mid-2009, at the same time prices for corn and wheat declined in response to large global supplies and continued weak demand.

There are other complications. In the case of soybeans, the world stocks data used to estimate the stocks-to-use ratio are measured at the end of the U.S. soybean marketing year. Because of seasonal differences in the southern hemisphere, that means South American stocks are estimated midway through their local marketing years.

Thus, the world stocks-to-use ratio is an imperfect indicator of market "tightness."

In the case of grains, China was a major player in the world stocks picture, especially before 2005. According to USDA statistics, China once held incredibly high levels of grain stocks; the USDA data suggests China once had a full year's worth of grain still in storage at the start of the next year's harvest.[7] USDA data and press reports reveal that China has sharply reduced those large grain stocks to levels more comparable to those in other countries. This policy change in China can explain, all by itself, much of the change in world stocks-to-use ratios over the last decade, and may be only loosely related to world market price developments.

The VeraSun Story

VeraSun was a very large U.S. ethanol producer until late 2008. The company used hundreds of millions of bushels of corn per year, so its corn purchasing methods had implications both for corn markets and for the company's bottom line. When corn prices rose to record levels in the summer of 2008, the company was concerned about both the price and availability of future corn supplies needed to operate its plants. The company took a series of positions in commodity markets that had the effect of locking the company into corn prices for fall 2008 delivery that proved to be far above the market price of corn. According to one press report, the company's average cost of corn for the third quarter of 2008 was between $6.75 and $7.00 per bushel, even as market prices for corn dropped to around $4.00.[8]

At the same time the company was locked into corn prices above cash market levels, the price of ethanol was falling because of the sharp decline in petroleum prices. The result was a severe squeeze on profits that contributed to the company's decision to declare bankruptcy. Many VeraSun ethanol plants were idled until buyers were found; as late as September 2009, several former VeraSun plants were still idle. The reduction in ethanol production meant less corn was being used, which put further downward pressure on corn prices. In other words, actions one firm took to try to protect itself against high corn prices set off a chain of events that pushed a major company into bankruptcy and depressed corn prices.

The Future of Speculation

Speculation will continue to play an important role in food markets, and people will continue to argue about the effect of speculation on food prices. Speculators can play both a positive and a negative role. On the one hand, they provide liquidity to the market. When there are more participants in the market, sellers will be able to find buyers and vice versa, and this moderates daily price movements. On the other hand, if speculators drive prices to levels inconsistent with market fundamentals, the results are disruptive.

Food markets involve a lot more than speculation in futures contracts. Options, swaps, and other tools are used to manage risk or place bets on future movements in food prices. These markets do not operate in a vacuum; governments set the rules of the road. New policies might limit who can participate in markets, restrict the stake any one individual or firm can hold in a particular market, or simply change reporting requirements.

Regardless of new rules, individuals and firms will continue to make decisions to buy and sell that will affect the future price of commodities. Those buy and sell decisions are based on imperfect information, so market prices for food will sometimes be higher or lower than they would be if everyone knew everything there is to know about the supply and demand picture. Speculation will be part of the story of food prices as long as the real world continues to be a messy place where much remains unknown or even unknowable.

Chapter 8

Stuff Happens

Any good mystery has an unexpected twist. In explaining recent swings in food prices, the investigation began by identifying a list of usual suspects—factors that have caused food prices to rise and fall in the past, and that will cause food prices to rise and fall in the future. Earlier chapters examined all of these usual suspects to determine which one or ones might have caused food prices to increase sharply and then decline between 2005 and 2009.

The investigation has concluded that *all* the usual suspects were responsible. The weather, economic growth, exchange rates, biofuel production levels, petroleum prices, government policies, and market speculation all played some role in both the boom and the bust in food prices. It would be tempting to declare the case solved, but there are still a few loose ends.

The problem is that the usual suspects are not the only guilty parties. There are many other reasons food prices rose and fell between 2005 and 2008. Some of these can be categorized and will repeat from time to time; others were one-time events. Stuff happens, and food prices rise or fall in response. This brings us to a final rule of thumb: *There will always be surprises that make it impossible to predict food prices with confidence.*

So what are some of these surprises? Avian flu, mad cow disease, and other animal diseases and food safety threats have caused sudden adjustments in food prices in recent years. Popular diet plans, such as the Atkins, Zone, and South Beach diets, can shift food consumption patterns. New technologies change the types of food available and affect the cost of producing and processing food. Sometimes the effects of these "other" factors on food prices are direct and obvious, and sometimes the effects are indirect and hard to discern.

The 2005–2009 Experience

It would be hard to exaggerate the importance of pork in China. In 2008, China produced and consumed about 46 million metric tons of pork—that's about 35 kilograms (77 pounds) per person (see Table 8.1). China produces more than twice as much pork as the European Union and more than four times as much as the United States. In fact, China produces more pork than all the other major pork-producing countries combined. The average person in China eats more pork than the average person in the United States, and per-capita pork consumption in China is rapidly approaching that of the European Union.

Table 8.1 *Pork Production and Consumption, 2008*

	China	European Union	United States
	(Million Metric Tons)		
Production	46.2	22.5	10.6
	(Kilograms per Capita)		
Consumption	34.9	42.7	29.0

Source: Author calculations based on August 2009 USDA estimates of pork production and consumption and U.S. Census Bureau estimates of population.

Within China, pork is the dominant meat. In 2008, China consumed about twice as much pork as beef, chicken, and lamb combined.[1] Compared to higher-income countries, Chinese consumers spend more of their income on food, and pork accounts for a higher share of consumer food spending in China than in most other countries. As a result, changes in pork prices have proportionally large impacts on the cost of living in China. When Chinese pork prices increase, it gets the attention of the public and policy makers far more than in Europe, North America, and other Asian countries.

Retail pork prices in China more than doubled between mid-2006 and early 2008, before retreating in the final months of 2008 (see Figure 8.1). This swing in Chinese pork prices was explained in part by income-driven changes in Chinese consumer demand, changes in feed prices affecting pork production costs, and other factors. However, another important part of the story is a hog disease commonly known as blue ear disease (more formally, porcine reproductive and respiratory syndrome, or PRRS). The disease spread rapidly in 2006 and 2007, killing large numbers of hogs before vaccination and other measures brought it under control.[2] This contributed to a reduction in pork supplies that helped to drive up pork prices.

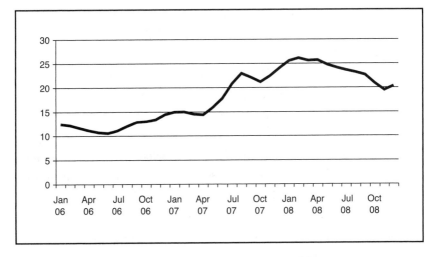

Figure 8.1   *Chinese retail pork prices, Chinese currency per kilogram*

Source: Data reported by the USDA's Foreign Agricultural Service in GAIN Report Number CH9017, March 2009.

While pork production in China and other countries changes cyclically, the decline in Chinese pork production in 2007 was particularly noteworthy. According to USDA estimates, 612 million hogs were slaughtered in China in 2006, but just 565 million in 2007. The result was an 8 percent reduction in pork production at the same time rising incomes were increasing consumer demand for meat in China.[3] Although blue ear disease was not the only reason for the decline in Chinese pork production in 2007, it was an important contributing factor.

The sharp reduction in Chinese pork production in 2007 had major implications for food markets. The increase in Chinese pork prices was the most direct and obvious result, but the effects spread to other food products and other countries, too. Reduced supplies of pork forced Chinese consumers to buy other types of food instead, pushing up their prices as well. The run-up in pork prices caused China to shift from being a net exporter of pork in 2005 and 2006 to a net importer by 2008. While the quantities involved are small relative to Chinese pork production and consumption, they are more significant relative to the modest amount of pork traded across country borders.[4]

The United States is a major pork exporter, and U.S. pork exports increased by more than 50 percent between 2006 and 2008. Increased U.S. exports of pork to China accounted for about 40 percent of the total increase in U.S. pork exports.[5] The sharp increase in world pork demand drove pork prices up in the United States and other countries in 2007 and 2008. Blue ear disease in China was one reason for that increase in worldwide pork prices.

High pork prices in China also set a number of other events into motion. Concerned about rising domestic food price inflation, Chinese officials offered subsidies and other programs to encourage increased pork production. High pork prices and these subsidies encouraged Chinese farmers to expand swine herds. The USDA estimated that Chinese pork production increased by more than 7 percent in 2008 and Chinese pork supplies continued to increase into 2009. As a result, Chinese pork prices in the final months of 2008 declined from their peak levels. With domestic supplies restored, Chinese demand for pork imports declined, contributing to lower pork prices in the United States and other countries.

The push to expand pork production in China also had important impacts on world crop markets. Soybean meal is an important component of hog rations in China and in other countries. To feed an expanding hog herd, the USDA estimates that China increased its consumption of soybean meal by 12 percent during the 2007/2008 marketing year.[6] Such a large increase would be noteworthy under any circumstances, but it was especially remarkable considering that world soybean meal prices increased by 64 percent in 2007/2008.[7] Chinese livestock producers could afford to use so much more soybean meal at a higher price because of high pork prices and government subsidies.

Whereas China has been largely self-sufficient in both grain and pork production in recent years, this is not true for oilseeds like soybeans used to make soybean meal. In fact, Chinese soybean production dipped slightly in 2007/2008, to 14 million metric tons. Meanwhile, Chinese soybean imports increased from 29 million metric tons in 2006/2007 to 38 million metric tons in 2007/2008. That 9 million ton increase in Chinese soybean imports accounted for the entire increase in world soybean trade in 2007/2008.[8]

At the same time demand from China was increasing, U.S. soybean production was reduced in 2007. U.S. farmers planted more acres of corn and fewer acres of soybeans, in part because of growing demand for corn from the ethanol industry. World soybean prices increased sharply in 2007/2008 in response to the increase in Chinese imports and the reduction in U.S. production.

In the final months of 2008, lower pork prices in China reduced the incentive to continue the rapid pace of expansion in the pork industry. As a result, the rate of increase in Chinese soybean meal consumption slowed. In addition, the reduction in pork imports by China had a negative effect on pork prices in the United States and other exporting countries. This slowed pork production growth outside China, too, further reducing the pace of growth in world soybean meal consumption. For this and other reasons, soybean meal prices retreated from their record highs in the final months of 2008.

Blue ear disease in Chinese hogs was not the only reason for all of these developments, but it was one contributing factor. With control measures in place, it appears unlikely that this disease will again have the same impacts on world markets. It is a reminder that unexpected things can and do happen, with important implications for food markets.

Why the Story Is a Little More Complicated

The full story of blue ear disease in China is not as simple as summarized here, and some of the facts remain controversial. For example, it is unclear just how many hogs died because of the disease. According to Chinese government sources, only 68,000 hogs died of the disease in the first eight months of 2007. Although that might sound like a lot of animals, it is not a large number in a country with hundreds of millions of hogs, and by itself would have had only a negligible effect on Chinese pork prices and world food markets. However, other industry reports suggest millions of hogs were affected and that blue ear disease was a major cause of higher pork prices in China in 2007 and 2008.[9]

Other animal health and food safety concerns have also affected food prices in recent years. Avian influenza decimated poultry flocks and endangered human health in Asia and elsewhere. Various measures limit trade in live animals and meat in order to reduce the likelihood of transmitting a variety of diseases. These measures can even turn into trade disputes, as countries argue about whether a particular restriction is truly intended to protect animal health and human safety, or whether it is just a disguised measure to protect domestic livestock producers by limiting competition.

In cases like that of blue ear disease in China, the immediate result of a disease outbreak is a reduction in food production that results in higher food prices. In other cases, concerns about food safety cause consumers to avoid affected products, which in turn results in lower prices for those products. For example, when some peanut products were recalled because of salmonella contamination in the United States in early 2009, some consumers avoided all peanut products for a time, even those not involved in the recall. The response to these outbreaks often set in motion a chain of events that affect food markets for weeks, months, or even years after the immediate crisis is resolved.

You could view these cases of animal disease outbreaks and food safety issues much like the weather. Everyone knows that there will be droughts, floods, hurricanes, and other weather events that will affect food production, but it is very difficult to predict when and where they will occur. Likewise, disease outbreaks and food safety issues are certain to happen from time to time, but it is almost impossible to predict precisely when and where they will happen.

An important distinction is that farmers, governments, and others in the food industry can take steps to reduce the frequency and severity of disease outbreaks and food safety problems.[10] Some of these steps affect food prices. For example, more rigorous regulation of food production and processing might reduce the likelihood of food-borne illnesses, but it could also increase the cost of producing food. In the end, consumers get safer food, but they also have to pay more for it.

Another Animal Disease Example

Another animal disease has attracted a lot of attention since the mid 1990s. Bovine spongiform encephalopathy (BSE, often known as mad cow disease) was first identified in the 1980s, but only in 1996 was it linked to a variant of a rare but invariably fatal human disease, Creutzfeldt-Jakob disease (CJD). Most BSE cases and most human deaths from the variant of CJD tied to BSE occurred in the United Kingdom.[11]

When the link between BSE and CJD was identified, concerns about the safety of eating beef caused a sharp drop in beef consumption and beef prices across Europe. The European Union took aggressive steps to control the disease. For example, all animals in infected herds were destroyed, and for several years all U.K. cattle over 30 months in age (those most susceptible to BSE) were also removed from the food chain. Over time, European beef consumption and prices recovered as control measures succeeded.

BSE was not identified in North America until a case was found in Canada in May 2003. The United States and other countries immediately shut their borders to imports of Canadian cattle and beef. This had major impacts on cattle prices on both sides of the border. In Canada, the loss of the U.S. and other foreign markets caused cattle prices to crash. Meanwhile, by reducing available supplies of cattle and beef in the U.S. market, U.S. cattle prices rose in the final months of 2003.

Then in December 2003, a case of BSE was discovered in the United States. Japan, South Korea, and other countries closed their borders to imports of U.S. beef, and the result was lower cattle prices in the U.S. market than had prevailed in late 2003. U.S. consumers as a group did not show much concern about eating U.S. beef. In fact, U.S. beef consumption and beef retail prices both actually increased in 2004.[12]

Other countries slowly relaxed restrictions on imports of U.S. and Canadian beef in subsequent years. Even in 2008, however, U.S. beef exports remained 25 percent below the 2003 level, as consumers in several important importing countries remained reluctant to purchase U.S. beef.[13] These concerns about U.S., Canadian, and European beef have benefited cattle ranchers in Australia, Brazil, and other beef exporting countries where there have been no recorded BSE cases. Although it has been years since the height of the BSE crisis, effects on world markets for beef and other meats linger.

Fish Stories

Fish and other seafood are a major part of the diet in many countries. Seafood prices are sensitive to many of the same factors that affect prices of other foods. For example, faster or slower economic growth and swings in exchange rates can affect patterns of world seafood trade and prices. Even changes in crop yields can affect seafood prices. Many fish, shrimp, and other aquatic creatures are raised in controlled environments and are often fed crop-based feeds such as soybean meal so that they can grow bigger and faster and in a smaller area. Thus when bad weather causes a small crop and high feed prices, the cost of producing farm-raised fish and shrimp also increases.

As in the case of livestock and poultry, fish are also subject to diseases that can reduce production and raise prices. In Chile, for example, infectious salmon anemia (ISA) has devastated production of farm-raised salmon. Chile has been the largest supplier of salmon to the United States, so these reduced supplies put upward pressure on salmon prices in the U.S. market.[14]

Seafood production can be severely reduced by the expansion of "dead zones," areas where excessive nutrients in the water ultimately cause waters to be devoid of oxygen, and thus unsuitable for most aquatic life. Dead zones in the Gulf of Mexico and elsewhere expand and contract from one year to the next, depending on the amount of nutrients deposited, wind patterns, and a number of other factors. Over the past five years, the average size of the Gulf of Mexico dead zone has been about 6,000 square miles. The 2009 Gulf dead zone was smaller than expected, and one scientist suggests the reason is that unusually strong winds at key times and places mixed more oxygen into the water.[15] A smaller dead zone generally means more gulf seafood production, again showing how the weather can affect food production and prices.

Overfishing can deplete wild stocks, driving fishing fleets to move to new areas or harvest different types of fish. This raises fish prices and changes the types of fish available to consumers. Governments and international agreements regulate the industry in various ways, limiting the types and amounts of fish that can be caught, the number and size of boats that can be used, and the times when fishing is allowed.

At the same time, governments also subsidize fishing in many countries. For example, many countries subsidize the use of diesel fuel used to operate boats. As with other types of food, governments operate some policies that increase production and reduce prices, and other policies that limit production and raise prices. Some of these policies are intended to insure the long-run sustainability of the world's fisheries; others are primarily intended to support the industry today.

Diets and Food Prices

Food prices are affected by a range of other factors that are hard to predict and that do not fit into the categories identified in earlier chapters. A new popular diet can increase the price of recommended foods and reduce the price of prohibited foods, at least until markets have time to adjust to the new demand patterns. A hot new item on fast food menus or in a best-selling cookbook likewise can drive up prices. It usually takes time for new technologies to become widely adopted, but sometimes a new way of producing or processing food can have an immediate effect on the cost of putting an old or new food product on a grocery store shelf.

Consider what would happen if large numbers of people simultaneously decide to follow strictly a low-carbohydrate diet, such as the Atkins or South Beach diets. Consumption of bread, cereals, rice, and other foods high in carbohydrates would decline, and this would put downward pressure on the prices of those and related items. In contrast, consumption of meat and other products low in carbohydrates would increase, resulting in higher prices for those food products. The ultimate effect on the price of a basic grain such as corn might be hard to predict, as reduced demand for corn to make corn chips might be offset by increased demand for corn as a livestock feed.

Shifts in food consumption patterns can both result from and cause changes in food prices. For example, consider recent changes in consumption of sugar and high-fructose corn syrup (HFCS) in the United States. Between 2005/2006 and 2007/2008, U.S. per-capita consumption of high-fructose corn syrup declined and consumption of sugar increased.[16] One explanation for these changes is that consumers have read stories suggesting HFCS is linked to obesity and other health concerns, so they are deliberately avoiding products containing HFCS.[17]

Another explanation, however, is that HFCS prices rose sharply between 2005/2006 and 2007/2008, both in absolute terms and relative to the price of sugar. For many years, HFCS was much cheaper than sugar, so soft drink manufacturers and other food processors had a strong incentive to use it wherever practical. When HFCS prices increased with corn prices, it was no longer such a bargain. Processors switched their use of sweeteners and advertised they now had an HFCS-free product to sell.[18]

More Surprises Ahead

It is safe to bet that there will be many more surprises ahead in food markets. Even if someone could precisely predict the weather, the state of the general economy, the price of oil, and government policies, there will always be some unexpected development that will affect the price of food.

For perspective, remember what the world looked like before the fall of the Soviet Union. Not only was the Cold War a major concern, but world food markets were very different than they are today. The Soviet Union was a major grain importer that needed to feed a large and heavily subsidized livestock sector. Now the successor republics as a group are major grain exporters. Feed consumption of grain has declined sharply because of reduced production of milk, beef, and pork.

Very few economists predicted this turn of events that has had profound effects on world food markets. After the fact, the story is easy to explain in terms of changes in government policy and consumer incomes. Disposable incomes fell in the immediate aftermath of the dissolution of the Soviet Union, contributing to a decline in consumption of meat and dairy products. Removing production and consumption subsidies further contributed to the shrinking of the livestock sector. Although rising incomes resulted in some growth in meat and milk consumption in recent years, animal protein production and consumption remain well below pre-1990 levels.

Although the story can be explained, that is not the same thing as saying it was easy to predict. Future surprises in world food markets may have nothing to do with political regime changes, animal diseases, or any of the other factors described in this book. The only thing that is safe to say is that we will someday say, "We didn't see that one coming."

Chapter 9

A Longer View

How will food prices evolve over the next few months, years, or decades? All the factors discussed in previous chapters are likely to have an impact on food prices far into the future. If favorable weather results in good global harvests, for example, food prices in any given year will be lower than if droughts in key growing regions reduce global crop supplies.

Future food prices will not depend only on things that make food prices change from one year to the next, but also on factors that cause food prices to change from one decade to the next. Population growth, for example, may not cause big annual swings in food prices, but it will be a critical factor in determining how food prices change between now and 2050. Likewise, new technologies do not normally result in large changes in food production and prices from one year to the next, but they can have big impacts on food markets in the longer run.

Before looking to the future, consider how food prices have evolved in recent decades. It is possible to look at the data and draw very different conclusions. Consider a very simple question: What has happened to the price of wheat since 1945? The answer is very different depending on whether or not you correct for overall inflation in the economy (see Figure 9.1). U.S. farmers received $55 per metric ton ($1.49 per bushel) for the wheat they produced in 1945 and $249 per metric ton ($6.78 per bushel) for the wheat they produced in 2008.

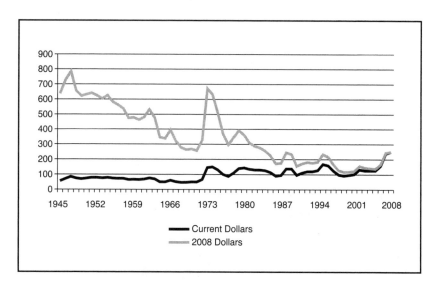

Figure 9.1 *U.S. farm wheat prices, dollars per metric ton*

Source: The wheat price in current dollars is the U.S. marketing year average farm price, as reported by the USDA. The price in 2008 dollars is computed by deflating nominal wheat prices by the U.S. consumer price index reported by the Bureau of Labor Statistics.

That is a large increase in wheat prices, but other prices in the U.S. economy rose even more rapidly. The overall consumer price index was 12 times as high in 2008 as it was in 1945—the average product that sold for $1 in 1945 sold for $12 in 2008. In terms of 2008 inflation-corrected "real" dollars, the price U.S. farmers received for wheat declined from $635 dollars per metric ton in 1945 to $249 in 2008, a decline of more than 60 percent. Prices for wheat and a wide range of other raw farm products have increased less rapidly than the general rate of inflation since World War II. Combined with rising incomes for most of the world's population, this means that basic staple foods have generally become more affordable to more consumers over time.

Most of the decline in inflation-adjusted wheat prices occurred in the 1950s and 1960s, a period of rapid growth in world food production. Crop production shortfalls, the first world oil price spike, and large purchases of grain by the Soviet Union contributed to dramatically higher prices for wheat and other grains in 1973. That food crisis led to widespread concern about whether the world would be able to feed itself, but in just a couple of years, real prices for wheat and other farm products resumed their long-term downward trend.

Prices for wheat, corn, rice, and many other farm products reached record levels in 2007 and 2008, and even inflation-adjusted wheat prices reached their highest levels in more than 20 years. This latest food crisis raised the question of whether this was another temporary spike caused by a combination of rare events, or if half a century of declining real grain prices had come to an end. Lower food prices in the final months of 2008 and 2009 alleviated some of the panic, and stories about food prices no longer appeared regularly on the front pages of major newspapers. Still, major questions remain about how food prices are likely to evolve in the years and decades ahead.

The list of things that will affect future food prices is long. Instead of trying to catalog them all, consider five major drivers of food prices in the long run: population, income, technology, energy, and policy. These five major drivers are certain to play critical roles in future food market developments.

Population

As the world's population grows, so does the demand for food. If supplies cannot keep pace with the increase in demand, food prices will rise. Population growth can explain most of the growth in world grain consumption over the last several decades, and it is certain to be a critical driver of food markets in the future. Thus, one important question is how fast the world's population is likely to grow.

The world's population doubled from 3.0 billion in 1960 to 6.1 billion in 2000. The United Nations estimates that the world's population could reach 9.1 billion by 2050 under a moderate set of assumptions (see Figure 9.2).[1] Exactly how fast the world's population will grow over the next several decades is uncertain, as it depends on everything from advances in health care to the average number of children who will be born to the next generation of women.

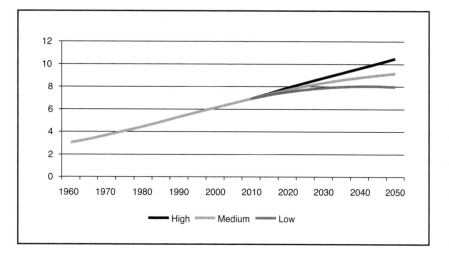

Figure 9.2 *World population, billion*

Source: United Nations World Population Prospects, 2008 estimates.

The United Nations reports that the world average fertility rate has declined from 4.9 children per woman in the early 1960s to fewer than 2.6 children per woman today.[2] The estimate of a 2050 world population of 9.1 billion people assumes that world average fertility rates will fall to 2.0 children per woman by 2050. The entire decline in projected fertility rates occurs in less developed countries, where the assumed fertility rate falls from 2.7 children per woman today to less than 2.1 in 2050. Fertility rates in developed countries are actually assumed to increase slightly from 1.6 to 1.8 children per woman.

The United Nations offers a range of future population estimates. A low estimate shows a 2050 population of 8.0 billion and a high estimate has the world's population reaching 10.5 billion in 2050. All of these estimates assume at least some further slowing of fertility rates in the future; they differ primarily in how much they assume fertility rates slow. If fertility rates remain at current levels indefinitely, the U.N. estimates the world's population would reach 11 billion in 2050.[3]

It makes a huge difference to world food markets whether the world's population in 2050 is 8 billion or 11 billion. Even the higher estimate, however, suggests that the annual percentage growth rate in the world's population will be lower in the future than it was between 1960 and the present. The U.N. medium estimate suggests that the annual growth in the world's population will decline from 1.2 percent in 2009 to 0.3 percent in 2050. In comparison, the world's population was growing by more than 2 percent per year in the late 1960s.

Another way of looking at the question is to consider the actual number of people added to the world's population each year. From 1980 to 2000, the world's population increased by an average of more than 80 million people per year. The annual growth has dipped slightly, but the world's population continues to grow by more than 75 million people per year. In the future, the U.N. medium estimates suggest that only about 30 million people will be added to the world's population in 2050. In the low estimates, the world's population actually shrinks after 2040. Only in the high estimate does the number of people added to the world's population each year remain near current levels.

If the world's population growth rate slows, it will be easier to satisfy world food demand and it should help to moderate food prices. In the 1960s, world food production had to grow by 2 percent per year just to hold per-capita consumption constant. To consistently achieve that type of growth requires rapid increases in crop yields or a significant expansion in the area devoted to crop production. In contrast, if world population growth drops below 1 percent per year, it might be possible to satisfy world food demand without requiring such rapid growth in supplies.

Population does not always grow at a steady rate. Wars, pandemics, and natural disasters can kill millions of people, and such catastrophes have huge impacts on markets for food. Anything that causes a sudden reduction in the world's population would reduce food demand, but some catastrophes can also disrupt the ability of the world to produce food and get it from farmers to consumers. Wars, for example, can make trade expensive or impossible, driving up food prices in countries reliant on food imports.

What matters is not just how fast the world's total population grows, but where that growth occurs. Because dietary patterns differ so much across countries, population growth in China may have different implications for world food markets than similar growth in India or Nigeria. In low-income countries, population growth primarily implies increased demand for basic staples like wheat, rice, corn, and beans. In higher-income countries, population growth also means increased demand for meat, milk, and other higher-valued foods.

Because people in China consume a lot more meat than people in India or Nigeria, population growth in China would be likely to have a larger impact on meat demand than would similar population growth in India or Nigeria. Thus, it is very important that population is expected to grow far more rapidly in Nigeria and India than in China.[4] Population growth is expected to be faster in low-income countries than in high-income countries.

Finally, it matters where population is growing, even within countries. In many low-income countries, large numbers of people are moving from rural to urban areas. Some of those people will keep the dietary habits they had in the countryside, but others will adopt at least some of the patterns common in their new communities. In parts of Latin America, for example, people in rural areas consume corn as their staple food, but people in urban areas are more likely to eat bread made from wheat. As the world becomes more urban, food consumption patterns will shift, with important implications for food prices.

Population growth will continue to be a major factor in world food markets. If current projections hold, however, it will not put as much pressure on food prices as it did in recent decades. Feeding a growing world population will always be a challenge, but slower rates of population growth may make the challenge more manageable.

Income

While the role of population growth in determining future food demand may be diminishing, the role of income growth will probably expand. People change how much and what they eat when their incomes rise. If an expanding world economy results in broad-based growth in incomes, the hungry will eat more and other people will increase the amount of higher-valued foods in their diets. The faster incomes grow between now and 2050, the more dietary patterns are likely to change. Economic stagnation or uneven growth that leaves many people behind could mean that world hunger persists for decades to come.

If there is considerable uncertainty about future world population growth, there is probably even more uncertainty around future world economic growth. The financial crisis of 2008 is a reminder that the world economy holds many surprises. Some would argue that longer-term growth rates are more predictable, but it is easy to find examples of countries that have grown much more rapidly or more slowly than expected over extended periods of time. For example, Japan followed decades of rapid economic growth with a long period of economic stagnation that surprised most observers.

In many middle-income countries, rising incomes have been associated with increases in consumption of meat, poultry, and dairy products. If this pattern persists, it could have huge impacts on global food markets. More cattle, hogs, chickens, and sheep are likely to eat more grain and oilseed meal. Even if changing diets reduce direct human consumption of grain, this effect is likely to be more than offset by increased animal feed use of grain. Livestock and poultry consume most of the world's corn, and oilseed meals are the primary source of protein in animal feed rations.

Consider the case of China, where pork production was four times higher in 2008 than in 1980 (see Table 9.1). Beef, poultry, and milk production grew even more rapidly. To feed all these animals, the amount of corn used in livestock and poultry feed rations quadrupled between 1980 and 2008, and soybean meal consumption increased at an incredible pace.

Table 9.1 *China Animal Production and Feed Use, Million Metric Tons*

	1980	1990	2000	2008
Pork production	11.3	22.8	39.7	46.2
Beef production	0.3	1.3	5.1	6.1
Chicken production	n.a.	2.4	9.3	11.9
Milk production	1.4	4.8	9.2	37.8
Corn feed use	27.1	53.4	92.0	110.0
Soybean meal use	1.1	1.0	15.0	31.8

Source: USDA's PSD Online, August 2009.

If incomes continue to rise in China, there will be further increases in Chinese consumption and production of meat, poultry, and milk. More grain and oilseed meals will be used to feed animals. The real questions are just how large these changes will be, and whether China will be able to satisfy increased food demand by increasing domestic food production. China may already have reached the point where each additional unit of income has a smaller effect on food consumption patterns, so it is likely that the pace of change in Chinese diets will slow. So far, China has been able to increase domestic food production rapidly enough that it normally does not rely much on imports of meats, dairy products, and grain. The main exception to this rule is the oilseed sector, where China is the largest importer in the world and a critical factor in world market developments.

China remains a major source of uncertainty in world food markets, but it is not alone. If incomes grow in other countries, they are also likely to see changes in dietary patterns. Every country is unique; rising incomes in India or Indonesia would result in different dietary changes than those in China. In India, rising incomes have led to increasing consumption of dairy and poultry products, even though much of the population avoids meat for religious and cultural reasons. In many countries, diets will change if incomes rise, and this will have important impacts on world food markets.

Dietary patterns in high-income countries also matter. For example, U.S. meat consumption per capita rose until 2004, but the combination of higher meat production costs and the 2008 recession caused consumer meat purchases to decline slightly from 2004 to 2009.[5] Future large increases in consumption of meat and dairy products in high income countries seem unlikely, given high current consumption levels, an aging population, and health concerns.

It is far from clear just how diets in high-income countries will change in the future. Will we adjust our eating habits to better match dietary guidelines? Will we continue to eat more and more of our food away from home? How will we weigh convenience relative to other concerns? Will the demand for organic and locally grown foods continue to grow? The choices we make will have major implications for our families and for the global food system.

Consider what would happen if U.S. consumers reduced their consumption of meat, sugar, and fats, and increased their consumption of fruits, vegetables, and whole grains. The increased demand for fruits and vegetables would result in higher prices for those products, which would encourage increased production and imports. Reduced demand for meat would result in lower livestock and poultry prices. Reduced profitability of livestock operations would eventually result in lower meat production.

The grain sector would see offsetting effects. On the one hand, direct human consumption of whole grain products would increase, and land shifting to fruit and vegetable production would reduce grain supplies, both of which would tend to increase grain prices. On the other hand, reduced meat and livestock production would mean less demand for grain as a feed, which would tend to reduce grain prices. It seems likely that this feed demand effect would dominate, so that the net effect of the assumed dietary shift would be to reduce grain prices. Sugar and vegetable oil prices would also fall because of reduced demand. Lower grain, sugar, and vegetable oil prices, in turn, would reduce the cost of the raw materials used by the biofuel sector, likely resulting in increased production of ethanol and biodiesel.

As important as dietary changes in high-income countries might prove to be, most of the world's population lives in low- or middle-income countries in Asia, Africa, and Latin America. The largest and most important changes in future world food consumption are likely to occur in these countries, not in the United States, Europe, or Japan. How fast and how broadly incomes grow and how consumers respond to more money in their pockets will have a critical effect on global food markets.

Technology

The way the world produces food is constantly changing. Although many basic practices have remained the same for decades or even centuries, every year there are innovations. New technologies are rarely the cause of major swings in food prices from one year to the next, but they do have large impacts on food prices over the course of decades.

One indicator of changing technology is world cereal yield growth since 1960 (see Figure 9.3). Adding up all the corn, wheat, rice, and other grains produced in the world, the average yield in the early 1960s was about 1.3 metric tons of cereal from every hectare harvested. That average rose rapidly over time, and first exceeded 3 metric tons per hectare in 2004. There is considerable annual variation around the long-term trend due to weather, crop and input prices, and other factors, but the upward trend has been remarkably stable over the past five decades.

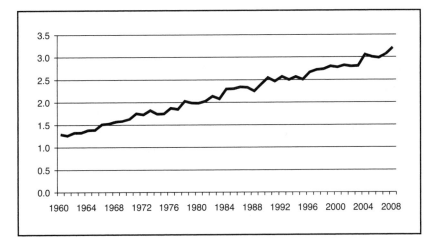

Figure 9.3 *World cereal yields, metric tons per hectare*

Source: Author calculations based on data in the USDA's PSD Online data set, June 2009.
Includes wheat, corn, rice, sorghum, barley, oats, millet, rye, and mixed grains.

Putting the same data in a slightly different context, the average world cereal yield between 2003 and 2007 was about 65 percent greater than the average world cereal yield between 1973 and 1977. Over that same 30-year period, the world population increased by 58 percent. The area devoted to cereal production actually declined slightly over those 30 years, so cereal production also increased by 58 percent. In other words, world per-capita cereal production was essentially unchanged, in spite of rapid population growth and no increase in the amount of land devoted to cereal production. This was only possible because of new technologies that made it possible to harvest more wheat, corn, rice, and other grains from every hectare.

The increase in world cereal yields cannot be attributed to any single factor. Public and private sector research led to the development of new seeds with higher yield potential. Fertilizer use was increased to provide necessary nutrients. Irrigation systems were expanded and improved to provide water at the time and in the quantities required. New chemicals controlled weeds and insects. New machinery let each worker cover more ground in less time.

The main benefit from all these changes is that the world is able to produce more food at a lower cost than was possible with 1960 technology. There have also been a number of negative consequences that critics are quick to point out:

- The new technologies require purchase of costly inputs.
- Fertilizer and chemical use can hurt water quality and endanger wildlife and the health of both farmers and food consumers.
- Excessive irrigation may come at the expense of other water uses and may not be sustainable.
- The development of new technologies has focused on a few crops and regions, and many farmers have been left behind.

- Because new technologies have contributed to increased food production and lower food prices, farmers who cannot profitably adopt the new technologies are often forced to leave the business.

- In many countries, the average farm size has increased and the number of farmers has declined.

Defenders of current technologies would be quick to argue that the concerns of critics are often exaggerated or simply incorrect. The key points are simply that technology has played and will continue to play an important role in world food production and prices, and that new technologies are often controversial.

While crop yields may be the most obvious indicator of the effects of technology in food markets, technology also affects other aspects of the food system. The average cow produces far more milk today than 50 or even 20 years ago. Livestock and poultry consume less grain for every pound of meat they produce. Food processors have developed new products that make food preparation easier and that have other characteristics that many consumers want. All of these technologies have impacts on food prices, and they also raise a range of societal concerns.

Not all consumers want foods developed with these new technologies, and many are voting with their pocketbooks by buying organic foods and other products that do not rely on technologies they consider objectionable. Typically, these alternative foods cost more to produce and sell for a higher price than conventional food products. If consumers continue to be willing to pay a price that lets farmers produce these alternative foods at a profit, they will continue to capture a growing share of the market.

How technologies evolve over the next several decades will have major impacts on food prices. For example, if crop yields can grow at the same pace they have for the last 50 years, it should be possible to increase per-capita production of grain and other crops without bringing more land into agricultural production. There are many challenges to achieving sustained growth in food production. Groups like the International Food Policy Research Institute have pointed out that public investment in developing new crop technologies has been lagging, and this could result in slower growth in crop yields and higher food prices.[6] Water resources have been stretched to the limit in many regions, making it difficult even to sustain current irrigation systems, let alone develop new ones. Erosion has depleted soils in many regions. Farmland has been converted to roads, factories, and shopping malls. Overfishing has depleted many types of marine life.

Technology optimists point to the steady growth in crop yields in recent decades and argue that any challenges can be overcome, just as they have been overcome in the past. Biotechnology gives researchers a new tool to boost productivity, they argue, and growth in crop yields could actually speed up in the years ahead.[7] Some new technologies are already in the pipeline, and more will be developed unless governments get in the way. Just helping other countries adopt technologies already available in high-income countries could result in sharp increases in food production.

If new technologies contribute to rapid increases in crop yields and livestock productivity over the next several decades, food prices are likely to be much lower than if productivity stagnates. If productivity growth slows significantly, it will be much more difficult to feed a growing world, especially if rising incomes result in more global meat consumption and high energy prices encourage increased biofuel production. The slower productivity growth is, the more land will be required to produce the same amount of grain and the more animals will be needed to produce the same amount of meat or milk.

Energy

The relationship between energy and food markets has become much tighter in recent years. Fossil-fuel prices have long had an impact on the cost of producing and transporting food, but the growth of the bio-fuel industry has added a new dimension. Biofuels provide a new source of demand for agricultural products, and this adds upward pressure on food prices.

Exactly how biofuels will affect food prices in the future depends on three major factors:

1. *Government policies.* Current U.S. policies require at least a certain amount of biofuel use regardless of market circumstances, and other countries have also established specific targets for biofuel use that are not tied to petroleum or food market circumstances. These policies could change in the future, with important implications for both food and fuel markets.

2. *The price of petroleum.* If the price of petroleum is high enough, there will be an incentive to produce and use even more biofuels than are required by current government policies. From 2006 to 2008, U.S. biofuel use exceeded government mandates, and it could happen again. If petroleum prices reach high enough levels, demand from the biofuel sector will result in a tight long-run relationship between crude oil and food prices.

3. *Technology.* As of 2009, the only commercially proven technologies to produce biofuels use grain or sugar to make ethanol and vegetable oil or animal fats to make biodiesel. Research is underway, and it is very likely that new ways of producing biofuels will become commercially viable, perhaps in the near future. Almost any imaginable process to

produce fuel from agricultural products will have some impact on food prices, but some processes will have greater effects than others.

To the extent that government policies largely determine biofuel use, the linkage between energy prices and food prices may not be very tight. Higher government-set biofuel use requirements will result in higher food prices by diverting more agricultural products to biofuel production, but energy prices will have little effect on biofuel production. In this case, food and energy prices will only be related because of the effect of energy prices on food production costs and the effect of biofuel production on prices for fossil fuels. Higher prices for fuel and fertilizer would increase farm production costs, with a negative effect on food production. This reduction in food production would, in turn, result in higher food prices. This effect may be of limited importance if energy prices remain well below 2008 peak levels.

If energy prices rise again and stay high for an extended period of time, the entire dynamic of food and energy markets could change. Higher oil prices increase the price that fuel users are willing to pay for ethanol and biodiesel as an alternative to fossil fuels. Higher biofuel prices, in turn, increase the profitability of biofuel production. While capacity constraints limit biofuel production in any given year, firms will build more capacity if they are confident the industry will be profitable. As the industry expands, the increase in demand for agricultural raw materials like corn, sugar, and vegetable oil will result in higher prices for those products. Farmers will shift away from other crops to produce more of the crops used in biofuel production and consumers will shift to more affordable foods. The result will be higher prices for a variety of food products.

For any given oil price, food prices can neither be so persistently low that biofuel production is extremely profitable nor so high that biofuel producers are all losing money. If food prices are too low relative to fuel prices, biofuel production will eventually expand until prices reach a level where plants are making a normal profit. If food prices are too high relative to fuel prices, biofuel production will contract until prices reach a level resulting in normal biofuel plant profits. In the long run, high fuel prices must result in high food prices, unless government policies actually prohibit biofuel production.

A key question is how energy prices are likely to evolve. The experience of the past few years shows just how difficult it is to predict future oil prices. However, consider the oil prices projected by the U.S. Energy Information Administration (EIA) in early 2009 (see Figure 9.4). The EIA projections suggest annual average oil prices in 2012 could exceed the 2008 record, and that prices could reach $180 per barrel by 2030.

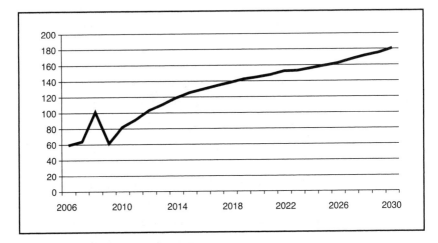

Figure 9.4 *U.S. crude oil import price, dollars per barrel*

Source: U.S. Energy Information Administration projections, March 2009

If oil prices rise to or above the levels in the EIA projections, it will probably be profitable to produce biofuels beyond the levels required under current law, even if no new technologies are developed. If this happens, the price of food could be largely determined by the price of oil. To oversimplify a bit, the price of oil will determine the price of food, the price of food will determine agricultural production and food consumption, and the biofuel industry will utilize whatever agricultural products are produced that are not consumed as food. The higher the price of food, the more agricultural production will occur, the lower the consumption of food will be, and the greater the use of agricultural raw materials in biofuel production.

New technologies could change the results, but the basic logic would still apply. Suppose, for example, that a new process can profitably produce biofuel from a crop not currently used for food production. This does not imply there will be no affect on food markets. More land will be devoted to production of this new biofuel raw material and less to food production. Unless this crop can only grow on lands that currently have no agricultural use, the new crop will displace at least some production of conventional crops or livestock, with resulting impacts on food prices. Production will continue to expand until it is no longer profitable to produce biofuels from this new crop. This may result in a very different crop mix than without the new technology, and the result may be a significantly larger increase in biofuel production, but markets for food and fuel would still be closely linked.

The linkage between fuel and food markets would only be fundamentally altered if someone finds a way to make very large amounts of biofuels from products that can be produced with essentially no impact on current agricultural production patterns. Although several candidates (corn and wheat plant residues and algae, for example) hold some promise of allowing significant biofuel production with minimal impact on food markets, none are currently commercially viable, and most have important secondary effects. Removing too much plant residue, for example, can reduce soil fertility and require increased fertilizer applications.

If energy prices stay far below 2008 levels, the linkage between food and fuel markets is likely to be weak, as government policies will be the main factor determining biofuel use and production. At high enough energy prices, however, the long-run linkage between food and fuel markets is likely to be very tight. High energy prices and low food prices just do not go together, at least not for very long.

Policy

Government policies will have important impacts on food prices in the future. Raising biofuel use requirements can result in more biofuel production and higher food prices. Even when oil prices are high enough that voluntary biofuel use exceeds legal requirements, government policies affect the relationship between food and fuel prices. Under current U.S. policies, each gallon of biofuel is subsidized, so this makes it possible for biofuel plant owners to pay more for each bushel of corn or pound of vegetable oil and still make a profit. These subsidies mean that, for any given crude oil price, food prices will be higher in the long run than they would have been in the absence of the subsidies.

While biofuel policies are critical, a range of other policies also affect food markets. Tariffs drive up food prices in the countries imposing the tariffs on imports, but drive down prices in other countries. Farm subsidies tied to current production levels benefit farmers and landowners in the countries providing the subsidies, but drive down food prices for everyone else in the market. Subsidies not tied to current production levels may still have important impacts on farmers and taxpayers, but are likely to have smaller effects on food prices.

Current and future rounds of trade negotiations are likely to have at least some impact on the rules of the road when it comes to tariffs, export subsidies, and even domestic production subsidies. Past rounds of trade negotiations have tried to reduce trade barriers and limit subsidies that have spillover effects on other countries. There is no assurance that future trade agreements will have the same goals or that those goals will be achieved. If future agreements do result in lower tariffs and subsidies, there could be important impacts on food markets. Lower tariffs would even out prices around the world for the most protected products. Prices would fall in the countries now imposing high tariffs, and rise in exporting countries and in countries that currently impose no tariffs.

Reducing trade restrictions has offsetting impacts on the volatility of food prices. On the one hand, consider a country that previously used trade barriers to isolate its food markets from the rest of the world. When a country reduces barriers and permits trade without restrictions, it finds itself exposed to the volatility of world markets. On the other hand, if a country experiences a domestic production shortfall or a sudden surge in demand, fewer trade restrictions mean an increase in imports can cushion an increase in domestic food prices. Some international markets, such as for rice, are notoriously volatile precisely because so many countries have policies intended to insulate them from world market developments. Reducing trade barriers could help reduce the volatility of world market prices, even if it has mixed effects on price volatility in the countries that relax their barriers.

Almost any trade agreement results in winners and losers, and the same can be said for most domestic government policies. Even policies that provide critical public benefits often harm some parties. Measures to increase food safety or promote animal welfare, for example, may be entirely justified even though they often increase production costs and contribute to higher food prices. Public food research investments may result in the development of new technologies that increase food production and lower consumer food costs. However, they also may harm farmers who cannot take advantage of the new technologies, and they incur a budgetary cost.

Finally, it is important to say a word about climate change. Global warming is not likely to have large impacts on agricultural production and food prices this year or next year, but it could be an important factor in food markets at some point in the future. This is not the place to review or debate the climate change literature, but many people believe it is very possible that 2050 food production and prices could be affected in important ways by climate changes. Food production could fall in some parts of the world and rise in others, and annual production and price volatility could change.[8]

The United States in 2009 was considering legislation that would cap future emissions of greenhouse gases and allow firms to trade the right to release carbon dioxide and other greenhouse gases into the atmosphere. Such a policy could have very major impacts on food markets for years to come. Climate change legislation is likely to raise the cost of fossil fuels, which would also increase food production costs.

Climate change legislation also could provide an incentive to farmers and others to find ways of removing (sequestering) carbon from the atmosphere. If farmers can get paid to sequester carbon, it could result in significant changes in production practices and patterns. Some of these changes, such as an increased use of farming practices that do not involve tilling the soil, might have only a small effect on food markets. Others could have much larger effects. For example, planting trees on land currently used for crop production or livestock grazing could sequester significant amounts of carbon. If farmers can get paid to plant trees on land currently used for food production, the result is likely to be higher food prices. More land for trees means less land to grow crops, reducing food production and raising food prices.

Three Alternative Futures

Each year, the Food and Agricultural Policy Research Institute puts together what we call our "stochastic baseline." It looks at 500 different ways that food markets could unfold over the next ten years by making alternative assumptions about annual weather patterns, the price of oil, and some of the other forces that affect world food markets. Even these 500 alternative futures do not exhaust the range of possibilities, because all the alternatives assume a continuation of current policies and hold a number of other key assumptions the same. Still, even this limited exercise shows that food prices can be much higher or lower depending on factors that are likely to vary in ways that are not very predictable.

Instead of trying to make sense of 500 or more alternative futures, consider just 3. In a steady-as-we-go scenario, food prices vary from year to year, but food price inflation is moderate and no greater than overall inflation in the economy. As farmers adopt new technologies, food production continues to expand, although at a slightly slower pace than between 1960 and 2009.

Food demand grows at a steady pace in this scenario, due to the offsetting effects of slower population growth and rising incomes. Lower population growth directly limits growth in total food demand, while rising incomes cause consumers in developing countries to consume more meat and dairy products. Moderate oil prices and a continuation of current biofuel policies mean that further growth in biofuel production does not put excessive pressure on food markets. Neither climate changes nor policies intended to reduce climate change have major market impacts.

A second scenario results in a world of rising food prices. Rapid income growth causes large increases in meat demand in middle-income countries, requiring more grain and oilseeds to feed more chickens, hogs, and cattle. This same economic growth increases the demand for fossil fuels, driving up oil prices. High oil prices push up the demand for biofuels, meaning more agricultural production is used to produce fuel instead of food.

Meanwhile, growth in agricultural productivity lags in this high food price scenario, both because of inadequate investment and public opposition to new technologies. Climate change, water scarcity, and other natural resource constraints make it harder to produce food. In trying to address climate change, policies encourage farmers to plant trees to sequester carbon, reducing the amount of land left to produce the world's food. These developments limit food supplies and boost demand for agricultural products, resulting in higher food prices. These higher prices may be affordable to those who benefit from economic growth, but increase hunger among those who do not.

A third scenario results in much lower food prices. Population growth slows, and economic growth rates in middle-income countries decline to rates more like those in the United States and Europe. Lower rates of income growth slow the expansion of meat demand in countries such as China, and aging populations in Europe and North America reduce meat consumption.

In this low food price scenario, slower economic growth, discovery of new oil fields, and conservation efforts all contribute to lower oil prices. Low oil prices and policy changes limit biofuel production to fuels made in ways that do not significantly affect food markets. New technologies are developed that allow farmers to increase crop yields even more rapidly than in the past. These developments boost food supplies and reduce demand for agricultural products, resulting in lower food prices.

The most likely outcome is that some forces will push up future food prices while other forces will push them down. Very different scenarios could actually result in very similar food prices. For example, the combination of slower development of new technology and slower growth in world incomes could result in about the same level of food prices as the combination of fast development of new technology and rapid growth in world incomes. However, it is unlikely that a world with very low income growth will have rapidly rising food prices, or that rapidly rising oil prices will coincide with declining food prices.

Final Remarks from the Author

The food price story is not a simple one. Biofuel production, energy prices, government policies, weather, income growth, exchange rates, market speculation, and a range of other factors affect how food prices change from one year to the next. All of those factors came together to push food prices up sharply from 2005 until early 2008, and then those same factors reversed course to push food prices back down again in the final months of 2008. Population and technology also affect longer-term trends in food prices.

This book does not come with a free crystal ball. If there is one thing I have learned in 20 years of making food market projections, it is that there is no way to know for sure what the price of food will be next year or in 2050. Nor do I presume to offer a prescribed list of government policies to support, stocks to purchase, or food to buy. Instead, my objective has been to help you develop a better understanding of some important aspects of world food markets so that you can make your own decisions with better information.

Appendix

Food 101

What Do People Eat?

Consumers visiting the local supermarket are offered a dazzling array of foods from all over the world. In spite of the diversity, an incredibly large proportion of the world's food is derived from a handful of basic crops.

There is no single best way to add up all the various foods in the world. It's not just a matter of comparing apples and oranges; it's also a matter of adding bacon, lettuce, and tomatoes; beer and pizza. One way to add up things that defy adding up is to focus on calories. The Food and Agriculture Organization of the United Nations (FAO) estimates the total amount of food available to consumers and converts it into calories (see Table A.1).[1]

Foods made from rice and wheat are central to diets, together accounting for more than one-third of all the calories directly consumed by the world's population in 2003. Other cereals, such as corn, sorghum, millet, and barley, are also important in some countries. As a group, foods made from cereals directly account for 46 percent of calories. Cereals are also used to feed animals providing the world's meat and dairy products.

Vegetable oils such as soybean, palm, and canola oil account for a surprisingly large share of total calories. In addition to their use in cooking oils and salad dressings, vegetable oils are key ingredients in a wide range of processed foods. Sugar and other sweeteners (such as high-fructose corn syrup) may have no other nutritional value, but they do

Table A.1   *World Human Food Consumption, Kilocalories per Capita per Day, 2003*

	Kilocalories	Share of Total
Rice	541	19%
Wheat	518	18%
Corn	152	5%
Other cereals	91	3%
Cereal total	1,302	46%
Vegetable oil	277	10%
Sugar and sweeteners	244	9%
Fruits and vegetables	154	5%
All other crop products	354	13%
Crop product total	2,331	83%
Dairy products	150	5%
Pork	119	4%
Poultry and beef	86	3%
Fish and other seafood	27	1%
All other animal products	95	3%
Animal product total	477	17%
Total food consumption	2,808	100%

Source: U.N. Food and Agriculture Organization, FAOSTAT website.

account for about 9 percent of calories. Fruits and vegetables provide a wide range of nutritional benefits, but as a group they only account for about 6 percent of total calories. Other crops of local or global importance include potatoes, cassava, dry beans, and peanuts. All of these crops combined contribute fewer calories than rice or wheat alone.

As a group, animal products account for 17 percent of total calories. Dairy products make the single largest contribution, followed by pork. In terms of global calories supplied, beef, poultry, and fish trail far behind pork. Other animal products include eggs, lamb, and mutton.

Other measures of world food consumption change the picture. For example, FAO reports that animal products accounted for 39 percent of the total amount of protein made available to people in 2003, more than double their share of global calories. Even in terms of protein, however, cereals remain very important, accounting for 41 percent of global protein available for human consumption. An indicator based on the market value of food consumed would result in a very different set of estimates, as it would place a heavier weight on fruits, vegetables, and meats, and would include products like coffee that are low in both calories and protein.

Whether focusing on calories, grams of protein, or some other indicator, global averages obscure the diversity of diets around the world. Relative to the global average, U.S. consumers eat more meats, dairy products, vegetable oils, sugar, and other sweeteners, and less rice. Chinese consumers eat more rice, pork, and eggs than the world average, but less sugar and dairy products. Meat consumption in India is very low, but dairy consumption is near the global average and cereals accounted for 59 percent of total calories in 2003. Corn accounted for 34 percent of total calories in Mexico in 2003, but rice consumption in Mexico was even lower than in the United States. Consumption patterns in Nigeria are a reminder of how much diets can differ around the world. Sorghum and millet are the major cereals consumed in Nigeria, cassava and yams are important calorie sources, and animal products accounted for a mere 3 percent of total calories in 2003.

Of course, countries differ not only in terms of *what* they eat but in terms of *how much* they eat. The FAO data suggest huge differences across countries in terms of total food consumption. In the United States in 2003, reported per-capita food availability was one-third greater than the world average; in India, it was 12 percent less. Within countries, food consumption patterns may differ more than they do across countries. Obesity and at the same time undernutrition are both common problems, even within the same country.

Cereals and vegetable oil accounted for much of the increase in world food prices between 2005 and mid-2008. Given the central role of these foods in diets around the world, many consumers have had few practical alternatives. Middle- and high-income consumers at least have the option of adjusting their purchases (eat out less often, avoid highly processed foods, etc.) to stay within a budget. Many poor consumers around the world have few options if they can no longer afford to buy even basic staple foods such as rice that supply a high proportion of their nutritional needs. Essentially, their choices are to eat less or to spend an even larger share of their limited incomes on food, reducing what they have available to pay for housing, education, health care, and other basic necessities.

What Do We Feed the Animals We Eat?

The world produces more corn than any other cereal, yet corn is a distant third in terms of per-capita human food consumption. The main reason is not the use of corn to make ethanol, but the use of corn as a livestock feed. About 500 million tons of corn are fed to hogs, poultry, cattle, and other animals each year, a quantity greater than all the milled rice people consume (see Table A.2).[2]

All the major cereals can be consumed by both people and livestock, but the actual patterns of use differ greatly across crops and across countries. In the United States, corn is primarily used as a livestock feed or processed into ethanol, high-fructose corn syrup, or a

Table A.2   *World Production and Use of Cereals and Oilseeds, Million Metric Tons, 2007/2008 Marketing Year*

	Production	Human Food, Seed, and Industrial	Animal Feed and Waste
Corn	792	274	496
Wheat	611	516	96
Milled rice	433	426	n.a.
Barley	133	42	92
5 other cereals*	152	84	66
9 major cereals	2,122	1,343	751
Soybeans	221	53	170
Rapeseed and canola	48	20	29
Cottonseed	46	5	27
Peanuts	32	19	8
Sunflowerseed	27	10	12
5 major oilseeds	375	108	246
Major cereals, oilseeds	2,496	1,451	997

Source: Author calculations based on the USDA's online data set, "Production, Supply and Distribution Online," September 2009.

*Sorghum, millet, oats, rye, and mixed grains.

variety of other products. In Mexico, most domestically produced white corn is used to make tortillas and other human foods, but rapidly rising yellow corn imports from the United States are used almost exclusively for livestock feed. Corn imports are also used for livestock feed in Japan and a variety of other countries in East Asia. China, second only to the United States in terms of corn production, uses about 70 percent of its corn as livestock feed.

In most of the world, wheat is used primarily or exclusively for bread, pasta, and other foods, but in the European Union, roughly half of all wheat is fed to livestock and poultry. Some of the world's barley is used to make beer, but about 90 million tons are used for feed. In Africa and India, sorghum and millet are used almost exclusively as human foods, but in the United States and Mexico, sorghum is primarily used for livestock feed.

Oilseeds, such as soybeans and canola, can be crushed to make vegetable oil and meal. Vegetable oils are used for human food consumption, biodiesel production, and a variety of industrial purposes, while oilseed meals are used almost exclusively as a high-protein feed for livestock and poultry. Soybeans, the dominant oilseed, are relatively low in oil content, so crushing soybeans results in a lot of livestock feed and a modest amount of vegetable oil. A small amount of soybeans is used to make tofu and other human foods and a similar amount is fed directly to livestock. Most other oilseeds are higher in oil content than are soybeans, so they produce a different mix of vegetable oil and protein meal.

Grains and oilseed meals are the primary feed for much of the world's livestock and poultry. Grains are a good source of calories, and oilseed meals are a good source of protein. Poultry generally require a high protein ration for maximum performance, so poultry rations usually include proportionally more oilseed meals than do hog or cattle rations. Like poultry, most of the world's hogs are also fed a ration that includes a balance of grain and protein meals.

By no means are grains and oilseed meals the only major feedstuffs. Most cattle and sheep primarily consume grass from the world's vast amounts of pasture and rangeland. In most of Europe and North America, dairy cattle are fed a ration that includes grains, silage,[3] oilseed meals, alfalfa, and other types of hay. In most of the world, beef cattle get almost all of their nutrition by grazing, but in North

America and a few other countries, most cattle are fed a ration high in grains in the final months before they are slaughtered. Growing in importance as a livestock feed are distillers grains and other co-products that are generated when ethanol is produced from corn. The world's livestock producers use many other feeds, ranging from kitchen scraps to fish meal, manioc, and citrus pellets.

Table A.1 demonstrated the central role of wheat and rice in human diets, but Table A.2 makes clear the importance of corn and soybeans in feeding the world's livestock and poultry. Many other crops are important, but wheat, rice, corn, and soybeans are well deserving of the special attention they receive in discussions of the world food situation.

Has Food Production Kept Up with Population Growth?

World food production and consumption have increased in recent decades. World cereal production and consumption have increased from less than a billion metric tons in the early 1960s to over 2 billion metric tons today (see Figure A.1).[4] In general, cereal consumption has grown more steadily than production, as weather and other factors can cause production to increase or decrease from one year to the next. In any given year, world cereal consumption can exceed world cereal production by drawing down inventories carried over from previous years. In the long run, of course, the world cannot consume food it does not produce, so the basic trend rates of growth in production and use are necessarily about the same.

The world's population increased from 3.0 billion in 1960 to 6.7 billion in 2008.[5] Most of the increase in world cereal production since 1960 has been needed just to keep up with the increase in population. Per-capita cereal production generally increased in the 1960s, but has

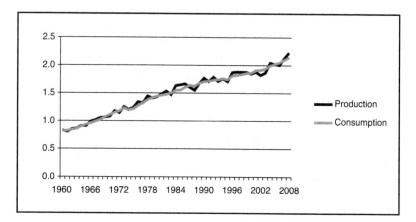

Figure A.1 *World cereal production and consumption, billion metric tons*

Source: Author calculations based on the USDA's online data set, "Production, Supply and Distribution Online," September 2009.

shown little trend over the past 30 years. Per-capita cereal production averaged 311 kilograms (686 pounds) per year between 1973 and 1977 and almost exactly the same between 2003 and 2007. This relative stability in the global figures masks a wide range of outcomes for different countries, cereals, and types of use. For example, in many countries, dietary changes mean an increasing share of cereal production is being used to feed livestock and a declining share is being used to produce food for direct human consumption. In recent years, ethanol production has accounted for an increasing share of grain use.

Production of other major foods has also increased dramatically in recent decades. World oilseed production has tripled since the 1970s. Sugar production has increased slightly more rapidly than the world's population.[6] Chicken meat production has quadrupled since the mid-1970s, while pork production increased by about 150 percent. In contrast, both beef and cow's milk production increased less rapidly than the world's population over the last 30 years.[7]

FAO reports that per-capita food consumption increased from less than 2,400 kilocalories per day in the 1960s to more than 2,800 kilocalories by 2003.[8] The percentage of the world's population under-nourished has declined over time, but the absolute number of hungry people has remained stubbornly high. Approximately 960 million people were undernourished in the developing world in the 1969–1971 period.[9] The latest FAO report estimates that 915 million people were undernourished in 2008, and that the total number of hungry people might exceed 1 billion in 2009.[10]

The increase in world food production in recent decades is in many ways an amazing success story. The world's population has increased rapidly, but world food production has increased at an even faster pace. By no means has this increase in food production solved all the world's problems, however. Increasing numbers of people around the world eat too much and a large number of people still do not have enough to eat. The title of the recent book by Raj Patel summarizes the seeming contradiction of a world that is both *Stuffed and Starved*.[11] Nevertheless, despite all the problems pointed out by Patel, Paul Roberts,[12] and other critics of the current world food system, the growth in world food production is still a remarkable achievement.

What's behind the Increase in World Food Production?

There are two ways to increase crop production. One is to increase the amount of land used to produce the crop, and the other is to take steps to increase the yield per unit of land. Over the last several decades, most of the increase in world production of cereals and oilseeds can be explained by increasing yields per acre or hectare.

Table A.3 compares average population and crop production figures for 1973 to 1977 to those for 2003 to 2007.[13] Between those two periods, the world's population increased by 58 percent, with an annual growth rate that declined from 2.0 percent in 1973 to 1.2 percent in 2007. Production of all four of the world's most important crops (corn, wheat, rice, and soybeans) increased even more rapidly than the world's population. Growing the fastest were soybeans and corn, the crops used primarily to feed livestock and poultry. Production of

Table A.3 *World Population and Grain and Oilseed Production*

	1973-77 Average	2003-07 Average	Change
	(Billion People)		
World population	4.09	6.46	58%
Production	(Million Metric Tons)		
Corn	338	709	110%
Wheat	373	601	61%
Milled rice	236	413	75%
Soybeans	61	216	252%
Other cereals and oilseeds*	380	435	14%
Major cereals and oilseeds	1,390	2,375	71%
Area harvested	(Million Hectares)		
Corn	122	148	22%
Wheat	225	215	-4%
Milled rice	140	152	9%
Soybeans	39	92	138%
Other cereals and oilseeds*	283	261	-8%
Major cereals and oilseeds	808	869	7%

Table A.3 *World Population and Grain and Oilseed Production*

	1973-77 Average	2003-07 Average	Change
Yield	(Metric Tons per Hectare)		
Corn	2.78	4.79	72%
Wheat	1.66	2.79	68%
Milled rice	1.69	2.71	61%
Soybeans	1.59	2.35	48%
Other cereals and oilseeds*	1.34	1.67	24%
Major cereals and oilseeds	1.72	2.73	59%

Source: Population estimates from the U.S. Census Bureau; crop estimates based on the USDA's data set, "Production, Supply and Distribution Online" September 2009, supplemented with FAO data.

*Barley, sorghum, millet, oats, rye, mixed grains, cottonseed, rapeseed, peanuts, and sunflowerseed.

other cereals and oilseeds grew much more slowly. In aggregate, total cereal and oilseed production increased by 71 percent.

The area devoted to producing some crops expanded while the area devoted to other crops contracted. Soybean area increased the most dramatically, due primarily to a huge increase in Brazil and Argentina. Corn area also increased substantially, while the increase in rice area harvested was modest. Wheat acreage actually declined slightly, partly because the United States shifted land from wheat to production of corn and soybeans. The total area devoted to other cereals and oilseeds dropped even more than wheat acreage.

Adding up all the major cereals and oilseeds, total area harvested did increase, but only by 7 percent. In countries such as Brazil and Argentina, the cropped area expanded at the expense of pasture land and other uses. In some countries, the practice of double cropping (harvesting two crops from the same physical unit of land in the same year) has increased, and this increases reported area harvested without actually bringing new land into crop production. In many other countries, the area used to produce cereals and oilseeds has been fairly stable, or has actually declined because of urbanization pressures and conversions of cropland to other uses.

Rising crop yields account for most of the increase in world cereal and oilseed production since the 1970s. Across all these major crops, yields increased from 1.72 metric tons per hectare in the mid-1970s to 2.73 metric tons per hectare between 2003 and 2007. This 59 percent increase in average yields almost exactly matches the increase in world population over the same period. The increase in yields can be explained by a wide variety of factors, including improved seeds, increased fertilization, more irrigation, and other changes in technology.

The increases in yields are very different across crops. Corn, wheat, and rice yields all increased proportionally more than the average of all cereals and oilseeds. Again, the causes are varied, but high levels of public and private research focusing on these major crops certainly contributed to rapid yield growth. In contrast, there has generally been less investment in developing new seeds and other technologies for crops like millet and sorghum, and yield growth for those crops has lagged. All else equal, higher yields translate into increased profitability, although this is not always true if the higher yields require greater use of more expensive inputs or if they result in lower prices for the final output.

Changes in crop yields not only explain most of the growth in total world crop production over the past several decades, they also explain most of the year-to-year variability as well. In any given year, the weather is the main factor explaining changes in crop yields. Droughts and floods can result in sharp reductions in yields, while ideal growing conditions can result in bumper crops. In any given location, production can be very sensitive to weather conditions. Yields on nonirrigated land in regions with variable rainfall (such as Australia and South Africa and even the U.S. Midwest) can vary dramatically from year to year. Global yields and production are less variable, in part because some regions have less annual yield variability and because unfavorable weather in one region of the world is often offset by favorable weather in another region.

What Role Does Agriculture Play in Different Countries?

In most high-income countries, agriculture today accounts for a small and declining share of the national economy. In the United States, for example, the share of production agriculture (farming and ranching) in GDP declined from about 7 percent at the end of World War II to less than 1 percent by 2002.[14] A relatively small number of commercial farms account for the bulk of agricultural production. Far more people are involved in transporting, processing, preparing, and selling food than are involved in farming.

The story in many low-income countries is very different. Half or more of the population may be directly involved in farming, and agriculture still accounts for a significant share of GDP. Farms are generally much smaller and less mechanized than in high-income countries, and a high proportion of food is consumed on the farms and in the rural communities where it is produced.

Table A.4 provides one indicator of just how varied agriculture's role in national economies can be. In most high-income countries, the agricultural population[15] is 5 percent or less of the total population. The share is significantly higher in the European Union than in the United States, Japan, or Canada, but that is primarily because the newer E.U. member states from Central and Eastern Europe are still much more dependent on agriculture than are countries in Western Europe. Note, for example, that the agricultural population is about

16 percent of the total population in Poland, but just 2 percent in neighboring Germany.

Table A.4   *Agricultural Population, 2006*

	Million People	Share of Country's Population
European Union	25	5%
Poland	6	16%
Germany	2	2%
United States	6	2%
Japan	3	3%
Canada	1	2%
Australia	1	4%
China	839	63%
India	585	51%
Indonesia	92	40%
Bangladesh	78	50%
Nigeria	41	28%
Congo	37	60%
Kenya	27	73%
South Africa	6	12%
Brazil	25	13%
Mexico	21	20%
Colombia	8	18%
Guatemala	6	45%
World	2,618	40%

Source: U.N. Food and Agriculture Organization, FAOSTAT website.

In contrast, the agricultural populations in most middle- and low-income countries are huge. In both China and India, the agricultural population accounted for more than half of the total population in 2006. The *agricultural* population of China was an astounding 839 million—greater than the *total* population of the European Union and United States combined. Even within regions, there can be great differences across countries. The share of the total population involved in agriculture in 2006 was six times greater in Kenya than in South Africa, and more than three times greater in Guatemala than in Brazil.

One final set of comparisons: The United States, Poland, South Africa, and Guatemala each had about the same agricultural population (approximately 6 million) in 2006. Kenya had a larger agricultural population than all four countries combined.

It makes little sense to speak of a "typical farm," even within a given country. In the United States and many other countries, most agricultural production occurs on a relatively small number of commercial farms. According to the 2007 Census of Agriculture, for example, 125,000 farms accounted for 75 percent of the value of U.S. agricultural production; the other 2 million farms accounted for the remaining 25 percent.[16] Even commercial farms are very different from one another. Many are family owned and operated; others have complex corporate structures and rely heavily on hired labor. In 2007, just 10,237 U.S. farms were owned by nonfamily corporations, and these accounted for about 6 percent of sales.[17] In many low-income countries, small-scale subsistence agriculture coexists with large-scale commercial agriculture geared toward urban and international markets.

How Important Is World Food Trade?

No country is completely self-sufficient in food. High-income Japan is one of the leading world importers of a wide variety of foods, including cereals, oilseeds, meats, and dairy products. Many low-income countries are also very reliant on imports of cereals and other basic foods. Most countries both export and import food, including countries that place a high premium on local production and self-sufficiency. Cuba, for example, is an exporter of sugar, but imports have accounted for more than half of domestic Cuban consumption of corn, wheat, and rice in recent years.[18]

The United States is a leading exporter of some food products and a leading importer of others. U.S. agricultural exports and imports both hit record highs in fiscal year 2008 (see Table A.5). Corn, soybeans, and wheat led the list of U.S. exports, but the U.S. also exported a lot of meat and dairy products. On the other side of the ledger, U.S. agricultural imports were dominated by processed and other high-value foods. Wine and beer, fruits and vegetables, and snack foods were among the top items imported.

Even within some product categories, the United States is both an exporter and an importer. For example, the United States exports fruits and vegetables to Canada but imports some of the same products from Mexico. The United States exports some types of beef and pork while importing others. Of the top U.S. agricultural imports, coffee and bananas are the only products with relatively little U.S. production.

The United States trades agricultural products with nearly every country in the world, but just a handful of countries dominate U.S. food trade. Canada is both the leading export market and the leading import supplier for the United States. Mexico and the European Union are also near the top of both lists. While China ranked fourth in both exports and imports in 2008, U.S. agricultural exports to China were more than three times as large as U.S. agricultural imports from China. Although China is a huge supplier of nonagricultural goods to the U.S. market, its role in U.S. food markets is relatively small.

International trade is much more important for some food products than for others. Among the major food crops, rice is at one end of the spectrum. The quantity of rice entering world trade is very

Table A.5   *U.S. Agricultural Trade, Fiscal Year 2008 (October 2007 to September 2008)*

Exports	Value ($bil.)	Imports	Value ($bil.)
Coarse grains*	15.8	Wine and beer	8.4
Soybeans	14.6	Fresh fruit	5.5
Wheat	12.3	Processed fruits, vegetables	5.3
Red meats**	8.2	Snack foods	5.2
Cotton	4.8	Vegetable oils	4.7
Dairy products	4.1	Red meats**	4.7
Poultry meat	4.0	Fresh vegetables	4.5
Processed fruits, vegetables	3.7	Coffee	3.7
Fresh fruit	3.6	Live animals	2.9
All other products	44.4	All other products	34.2
All agricultural products	115.5	All agricultural products	79.3
Canada	16.2	Canada	17.9
Mexico	15.6	European Union	15.8
Japan	13.1	Mexico	10.8
China	11.2	China	3.4
European Union	10.7	Indonesia	2.7
All other countries	48.6	All other countries	28.7
All countries	115.5	All countries	79.3

Source: Author calculations based on the USDA's online "BICO" data set, March 2009.

*Primarily corn, but also including sorghum, barley, and oats.

**Primarily beef and pork.

small relative to world rice production and consumption. In 2007/2008 for example, only about 7 percent of the world's rice production was traded internationally.[19] China, India, Indonesia, Bangladesh, and Japan are all countries where rice dominates the food economy, but exports and imports tend to be small relative to production and consumption. Many Asian countries equate food security with self-sufficiency in rice production, so they employ a range of policies to ensure adequate domestic production of rice and discourage imports. This "thinness" of world rice trade means that even mild changes in supplies on the world market can cause large swings in prices.

Soybeans are at the other end of the spectrum. In 2007/2008, approximately 36 percent of the world's soybean crop was exported as raw soybeans. An additional amount of soybeans was exported in the form of processed protein meal and vegetable oil, meaning that more than half of all soybeans produced in the world was exported as soybeans or soybean products.[20] Argentina is one of the three main exporters in the word, and the country exports almost all of the soybeans it produces, primarily in the form of processed protein meal and vegetable oil. China, on the other hand, is the dominant player on the import side of the soybean market. Although China has attempted to remain relatively self-sufficient in grain production, it has been willing to greatly expand its soybean imports to produce protein meal for a growing livestock population and vegetable oil for direct human consumption.

Patterns of world food trade change over time because of both short-term and long-term factors. The former Soviet Union was a major grain importer; indeed, a sharp increase in Soviet grain imports contributed to a previous major spike in food prices in the early 1970s. A sharp reduction in domestic consumption because of smaller livestock herds has made it possible for Russia and Ukraine to be significant grain exporters in most recent years. The weather, macroeconomic developments, and a wide range of other factors can cause agricultural product trade to change dramatically from one year to the next.

With all those caveats in place, it may be useful to briefly summarize recent patterns of trade for a few key food items:

- The United States is the dominant corn exporter, accounting for more than half of all corn exports. Argentina is the only other consistent large exporter, although Brazil has emerged in recent years. Japan is the single largest importer of corn, and Mexico is also near the top of the list of corn importers. The European Union is generally not a major player in world corn markets, although it was a large importer in 2007/2008. China is the second largest producer of corn in the world, and from 1985 to 2006 it was usually a corn exporter. An important question for the future is whether China might become a major corn importer to feed a growing livestock population.

- The United States is also the largest exporter of wheat, although it faces much more competition in world wheat markets than in the corn market. Canada, Australia, the European Union, and Argentina are all major exporters. No countries dominate the import side of the world wheat picture, although Brazil, Egypt, Japan, and Algeria are among the diverse set of wheat importing countries. China and India are both major producers and consumers of wheat. Although their exports and imports are generally small relative to their domestic production, they can have a major world market impact when they have surpluses to dispose of or shortages to fill.

- While world trade in rice is relatively limited, Thailand, Vietnam, the United States, India, and Pakistan are usually the main suppliers to the world market. The list of rice importers is very long, with the Philippines and Nigeria appearing as significant importers in recent years.

- In addition to Argentina and China, the other major players in the world soybean market are Brazil and the United States as exporters and the European Union as an importer. Brazil has brought large amounts of new land into production in recent years to increase its production and exports of soybeans.

- The United States is a major exporter of beef, pork, and poultry meat, as is Brazil. Australia and New Zealand are large beef exporters, and the European Union and Canada are significant exporters of pork. Japan and Russia are major importers of beef, pork, and poultry meat, and Mexico is an important market for the United States for all the meat categories.

- New Zealand, Australia, and the European Union are major exporters of dairy products, and Japan and Russia are major importers. The United States is primarily an importer of cheese, but is also an exporter of other dairy products.

- Brazil dominates world sugar exports. Once a significant exporter, policy changes mean that the European Union now imports more sugar than it exports. Cuba's role in world export markets has diminished, while India and Thailand have become important exporters. The United States and Russia are major importers, but as with several other food products, the list of importing countries is much longer than the list of exporters.

World trade patterns can change rapidly, so more precise descriptions would have a short shelf life. Annual outlook publications from the Food and Agricultural Policy Research Institute (FAPRI), the Organization for Economic Cooperation and Development (OECD), the Food and Agriculture Organization (FAO), and the U.S. Department of Agriculture (USDA) provide up-to-date estimates and projections.

Why Are Biofuels Getting So Much Attention?

Rapid growth in biofuel production has fundamentally changed world food markets. Just a few years ago, experts trying to predict food prices were very focused on the future relative rates of growth in food production and consumption. Although these prospects remain important and uncertain, new critical questions are how much agricultural production will be used for biofuel production, and with what impacts on food markets. Can we produce both food and fuel, or must we choose one or the other?

Biofuel production is not a completely new phenomenon; both the United States and Brazil have been producing ethanol for decades. What caught many analysts off guard was just how fast biofuel production has risen in recent years. In the United States, for example, ethanol production grew from 3.9 billion gallons (15 billion liters) in 2005 to 9.2 billion gallons (35 billion liters) in 2008.[21]

The sharp increase in U.S. ethanol production has required a corresponding increase in the amount of corn used to produce ethanol, growing from less than 15 percent of the U.S. corn crop in the 2005/2006 corn marketing year to 23 percent in 2007/2008 and approximately 30 percent in 2008/2009 (see Figure A.2). The United States now uses more corn to make ethanol than it exports, and the United States is the world's largest exporter of corn. As a share of world cereal production, U.S. corn use for ethanol production increased from less than 1 percent in 2001/2002 to more than 4 percent by 2008/09.[22]

Corn-based ethanol in the United States is not the only important story. Brazil has expanded sugar-based ethanol production, and the European Union has greatly increased production of biodiesel made

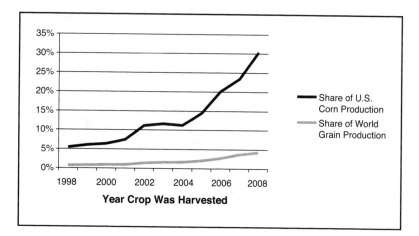

Figure A.2 *U.S. use of corn to make ethanol*

Source: Author calculations based on USDA data sets, including "World Agricultural Supply and Demand Estimates," September 2009.

from vegetable oils. A long list of countries around the world have started or at least considered biofuel projects.

In the United States, corn is the major feedstock for ethanol production. The starch in a kernel of corn is fermented to produce ethanol and the rest of the kernel is used to produce other products. In the most common type of U.S. ethanol plant, the main co-product of ethanol production is distillers grains, a livestock feed made from the portions of the corn kernel that cannot be turned into ethanol using current technologies. For every 56-pound bushel of corn, a typical ethanol plant in 2009 produces about 2.75 gallons (10.4 liters) of ethanol and about 17 pounds of distillers grains. In Brazil, sugarcane is used to produce ethanol. The juice from the sugarcane is fermented, and each metric ton of sugarcane can produce about 80 liters of ethanol.

In the United States, ethanol is typically blended with conventional gasoline, and the most common blend in 2009 is a 10 percent ethanol blend. In Brazil, standard fuel contains more than 20 percent ethanol, and the ethanol percentage varies from year to year. Specially equipped vehicles can operate with higher ethanol blends. In the United States, some vehicles can use E-85, a fuel blend that may contain up to 85 percent ethanol. In Brazil, most vehicles sold in recent years can run on pure ethanol or on gasoline-ethanol blends. Brazilian drivers can and do choose which product to put in their tanks depending on relative fuel prices, keeping in mind that a gallon or liter of ethanol only contains about two-thirds the energy of the same volume of gasoline.

In the European Union, United States, and several other countries, biodiesel is produced from vegetable oil or animal fats. Biodiesel has about the same mass as the original feedstock. Biodiesel production does not utilize the non-oil portion of oilseeds, so the same amount of protein meal is available whether vegetable oil is used to make biodiesel or sold into the food market. Biodiesel is typically blended with regular diesel fuel in relatively small proportions, but higher blends can also be used.

Biofuel markets are developing rapidly, and new technologies could result in major changes in the ways that biofuels are produced and used. Government policies will almost certainly have a major impact as well. Biofuel production is supported by a wide range of government policies in many countries, ranging from direct subsidies to requirements that a certain amount of biofuels be utilized, and these policies could change. Throw in underlying uncertainty about the future of crude oil prices, and it is very difficult to say with confidence just what the biofuel sector will look like in the years ahead. However, it is safe to say that biofuel developments will continue to have important implications for food prices.

Where Does the Consumer's Food Dollar Go?

Food is a lot more than the raw commodities (grains, oilseeds, and so on) sold by farmers. When consumers go to a supermarket or a restaurant, the money they spend supports the entire food system. In high-income countries, the share of the consumer's food dollar that actually finds its way back to farmers is relatively small. In 2007, for example, U.S. consumers spent about $1.1 trillion on food.[23] In that same year, the total value of all the crop and livestock sales by U.S. farmers and ranchers was less than $300 billion, and that includes commodities sold to other farmers or exported.[24]

Of every dollar that U.S. consumers spent on food in 2006, only about 19 cents went to farmers (see Figure A.3). In fact, the single largest component of the consumer food dollar is not the cost of raw farm commodities, but the wages and salaries of all the people involved in getting food from the farm to supermarket shelves and restaurant tables. These post-farm labor costs accounted for more than 38 cents of the U.S. consumer food dollar. Other important cost categories include packaging, energy, and transportation. Food industry profits accounted for about 4.5 cents of every U.S. consumer food dollar in 2006.[25]

These figures are averages across all the foods consumed in the United States, and the picture can be very different depending on the type of food and where it is purchased. Almost half of U.S. consumer food spending in 2007 was for food consumed away from home.[26] The share of the restaurant food dollar that is explained by the prices of raw farm commodities is generally quite low, and labor costs are a very large share of the final bill.

For food consumed at home, the story is very different for different types of food. According to USDA, the farmer's share of the con-

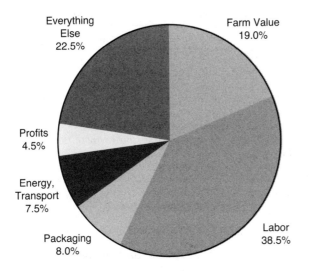

Figure A.3 *The U.S. consumer food dollar, 2006*

Source: Author calculations based on USDA Economic Research Service data.

sumer food dollar is generally between 25 percent and 30 percent for fresh fruits and vegetables, dairy products, and pork. Beef is one of the few food categories where the farm share exceeds 40 percent. In contrast, for cereal and bakery items, the farm value is only about 6 percent.[27]

Because raw farm commodities generally account for such a small share of U.S. consumer food spending, large changes in farm commodity prices may have only modest impacts on consumer food prices. As interest groups representing farmers are quick to point out, even doubling the price of wheat only increases the cost of producing a loaf of bread or a box of breakfast cereal by a few pennies.

The fact that farm commodities account for a modest share of the consumer food dollar helps explain why U.S. consumer food prices increased by *only* 5.5 percent in 2008. One measure of U.S. farm-level prices increased by about 10 percent in 2008.[28] If the farm value of the consumer food dollar is about 19 percent, that suggests the increase in farm commodity prices could directly account for about a 2 percent increase in consumer food prices in 2008. The full story is, of course, a lot more complicated. Higher energy costs, for example, also contributed to 2008 food price inflation by increasing the cost of transporting, processing, and packaging food.

Some might be tempted to conclude that higher farm commodity prices are not that important from a consumer point of view. That would be a mistake. Higher market prices for grains and oilseeds may only make a small direct contribution to U.S. consumer food price inflation, but they do make a difference. In the longer run, higher prices for corn, soybeans, and other feeds will eventually result in higher prices for meat and dairy products, and these higher prices will be passed on to consumers.

The discussion so far has focused on the United States, but it would be broadly true for middle- and high-income consumers around the world. The picture may be very different for the world's poor. The poorest people in low-income countries get most of their nutrition from basic staples such as grains and vegetable oils. When prices of those products increase as sharply as they did in 2008, the poor are likely to experience a much greater proportional increase in food prices than are high-income consumers.

What Government Policies Affect Food Prices?

Governments maintain a wide range of policies that affect the food sector. Quite often, the same government operates one set of policies that have the effect of raising food prices and another set of policies that have the opposite effect. Likewise, many policies have one effect on food prices in the country operating the policy, and the opposite effect on food prices in other countries.

Table A.6 summarizes a few of the major types of policies that affect food prices. Trade policies have direct and fairly obvious impacts on domestic food prices. Tariffs and other restrictions on imports mean that domestic consumers do not have access to food at prices available on world markets. These policies are generally designed to protect the domestic food industry, but they have the effect of raising food prices for both food producers and consumers.

Table A.6 *Effect of Government Policies on Food Prices*

	Domestic Food Prices	Food Prices in Other Countries
Tariffs and other import restrictions	Higher	Lower
Export subsidies	Higher	Lower
Payments to farmers		
Criteria tied to current production	Lower	Lower
Not tied to current production	Small	Small
Farm input subsidies	Lower	Lower
Land retirement programs	Higher	Higher
Public stock management	More stable	More stable
Biofuel mandates and subsidies	Higher	Higher
Food price ceilings	Lower	Higher
Domestic food assistance subsidies		
Effect on beneficiaries	Lower	Not relevant
Effect on rest of population	Higher	Higher
Research and education	Depends	Depends

The reduction in imports that results from tariffs and other import restrictions not only increases food prices in the country imposing the restriction, it also reduces food prices in other countries. When exporting countries cannot sell as much food to other countries, the result is lower prices for products traded in international markets. This price decline occurs not just in countries that lose export sales, but also in countries that now can pay a lower price for imported food. The magnitude of these price effects depends on the relative size of the country imposing the trade barrier and a variety of other factors. A small country imposing a tariff, for example, can drive up domestic food prices, but cannot have a meaningful effect on food prices in other countries.

A few countries subsidize food exports, making food available to foreign buyers at lower prices than would otherwise be available. These policies are far less common than import tariffs, but have been used to dispose of food surpluses and protect domestic food industries. The effects of export subsidies, in fact, are very similar to the effects of import tariffs: They raise prices in the domestic market and reduce prices in other countries.

In addition to policies that directly target trade, many high-income countries operate programs that make payments directly to farmers for a variety of purposes. At least some of these programs make payments that depend directly on how much a farmer produces. These types of policies encourage increased food production, and the result is lower food prices in both domestic and international markets.

Other programs make payments to farmers in ways that are not so directly tied to how much a farmer produces. For example, both the European Union and United States have programs that make payments that do not require farmers to grow any crops at all. These programs are much less likely to have large impacts on food production and prices than are programs that require farmers to produce a crop to get a payment. Programs that pay farmers to protect or enhance the environment generally would have only small impacts on food prices unless they result in significant changes in food production.

Farm input subsidies take various forms. Several governments subsidize the production or purchase of fertilizer, for example. The resulting increase in fertilizer use generally results in at least some increase in crop production and lower food prices. Likewise, many governments provide subsidized credit to farmers, which also results in more food production and lower prices.

Several countries also operate various types of land retirement programs. Some of these are temporary programs that only idle land for one season at a time; others retire land for a ten-year period or longer. The programs have a variety of purposes, ranging from supply management to environmental enhancement, such as reducing soil erosion or improving wildlife habitat. Regardless of the purpose, these programs generally result in some reduction in food production, which results in higher food prices both at home and abroad.

In the past, many countries operated buffer stock programs. By encouraging or requiring storage of grain and other food commodities, these programs were designed to boost food prices when there were surpluses and reduce food prices when there were shortages. Some of these programs worked better than others, and almost all involved considerable government expense. While buffer stocks were once maintained by the United States and other major countries, such programs are smaller and less common today.

Biofuel policies also have important impacts on food markets. Subsidizing biofuel production or requiring biofuel use results in more use of grains, sugar, vegetable oil, and the other agricultural products used to produce biofuels. This increase in demand for agricultural commodities results in an increase in food prices.

Many countries operate policies to reduce the cost of food to at least a portion of the population. Formal price ceilings are intended to cap food prices, but often have a variety of unintended consequences. Without other supportive policies, price ceilings can cause food shortages, as producers may be unable or unwilling to supply food at the ceiling price, and consumers may want to buy more food than is available at the government-set price. Responses to shortages induced by price ceilings include food ration systems and black market activity.

Besides price controls, many countries directly subsidize food to some portions of the population. In the United States, for example, the Supplemental Nutrition Assistance Program (SNAP, formerly known as food stamps) provides low-income individuals with benefits tied to the cost of a frugal diet. These policies reduce the cost of food to some consumers, which results in more consumption of at least some types of food. This increase in consumption, in turn, results in at least a slight increase in food prices for other consumers.

Finally, many governments support agricultural research and education. When these programs succeed in developing and disseminating new technologies that increase food production, the result is lower prices in both domestic and international food markets. Not all agricultural research is designed to increase food production, of course; indeed, much research is geared to finding new uses for agricultural products. If research leads to more nonfood use of agricultural production, the result can be higher, not lower, food prices.

This brief survey of government policies is incomplete and oversimplified. It should be clear, however, that governments have complicated and contradictory effects on food prices.

What Do Food Prices Have to Do with World Hunger?

World hunger is the result of a very complex set of factors and no one should pretend it is easy to correct or even define the problem. Take what might appear to be an easy question: Are people hungry because food prices are too high or because they are too low? At the risk of sounding like an economist, the honest answer is, "It depends."

It might seem obvious to conclude that high food prices cause hunger by pricing food out of the reach of the world's poor. Indeed, FAO's count of the world's hungry increased in 2007 and 2008 when world food prices were increasing. For many of the world's poor, rising food prices made it impossible to buy the food they needed to provide an adequate diet for their families.

Yet the full story is a little more complicated. Consider three low-income individuals whose families are at risk of hunger (see Table A.7). Christina is an urban worker in an industry unrelated to agriculture whose income is just enough to provide her family a simple diet. Ben is a poor farmer who sells some of the food he produces to pay for nonfood necessities. Maria is also a farmer, but she produces only enough food to feed her family and has an off-farm job to pay for other family expenses.

Table A.7 *Food Price Effects on Hunger: Three Examples*

	Characteristics	Effect of Higher Food Prices
Christina	Poor urban resident not employed by food industry	Increase hunger
Ben	Farmer producing much more food than his family consumes	Reduce hunger
Maria	Farmer who produces only as much food as her family consumes	Neutral or uncertain

Now consider what happens to each of these families when food prices increase. Christina's family may slide into hunger, as the rising cost of food is beyond the family's limited means. Food may account for half or more of her family's spending, so an increase in food prices may force her to make impossible choices between providing her family with adequate food and satisfying other basic necessities. The sharp rise in food prices in 2007 and 2008 severely affected people like Christina and their families. The increase in world cereal prices may have been an annoyance for high-income consumers who buy prepared and processed products and who spend less than 10 percent of the their income on food. It was a tragedy for people who get most of their nutrition from precisely the cereals that increased the most in price and who spend most of their income on food.

Ben's family may have a very different experience. When food prices increase, his income will increase. How he spends this money depends on his particular circumstances and preferences, but it's at least possible that he might spend some of the additional income on foods he would not otherwise have been able to afford. The quality of his family's diet may actually improve when food prices increase.

If Ben expects food prices to remain high, he may make investments that will increase his ability to produce more food in the future. If these investments prove wise, his future income will increase even more, meaning the family may be less at risk of hunger. In many poor countries, most poverty is concentrated in rural areas. If most of the people in rural areas are farmers like Ben, higher food prices may reduce poverty and hunger.

However, it would be wrong to conclude that higher food prices always increase hunger in urban areas and reduce hunger in rural areas. Maria only produces enough food to feed her family. Perhaps she occasionally has a small surplus that she can market, but the income is typically just enough to cover the cost of the foods she cannot produce herself. For Maria, higher food prices may have little direct effect on her family's ability to obtain an adequate diet; the weather and all the other factors that affect the harvest may be a lot more important.

Even in low-income countries where a high percentage of the population is directly engaged in agriculture, many people in rural areas buy more food than they sell. Thus, higher food prices may increase the income and food security of some families, while making it much harder for others to obtain the food they need.

The story is further complicated by food price effects on employment. In rural areas, higher food prices may mean more agricultural production and employment. An employed person is more likely to be able to feed her family than someone who is unemployed, even if food prices increase. The opposite effect may occur in urban areas. Because higher food prices leave families with less money to spend after covering food needs, businesses not related to food and agriculture sell fewer goods and services. This may eventually translate into fewer jobs and less household income.

Finally, it's important to say a word about "world food prices." It is common to speak as if everyone in the world pays the same price for food. They do not. One reason is that tariffs and other policies drive a wedge between prices in exporting and importing countries. In some cases, countries prohibit or strictly limit the amount that can be traded, and this has the effect of isolating the local food market from developments in the rest of the world.

The most important trade barrier, however, is often not a formal government policy, but rather the high cost of transporting food from and to remote areas. Difficult topography, poor roads, and long distances to ports can mean that it can cost more to move food from an exporting country to a final consumer than the initial cost of the food itself.

Whether local food markets become isolated from the rest of the world by policies or by transportation costs, the consequences for local food prices are mixed. On the one hand, swings in world market prices may have little or no direct effect on local food markets, so one source of food price variability may be removed or at least lessened. However, consider what happens when there is a severe drought that severely reduces local food production. Food prices may rise sharply and there may be no easy way to avoid hunger and starvation. Isolated markets are insulated from shocks that originate elsewhere, but local shocks will have larger effects.

In April 2009, FAO reported that despite the sharp decline in "world" food prices from their mid-2008 peak, local food prices in many low-income countries had not declined at all. For cereals, for example, domestic prices were higher than a year ago in 80 percent of countries.[29] This occurred even though the U.S. export prices for wheat and corn were much lower in March 2009 than in March 2008. Over time, more of the changes in internationally traded prices may well be reflected in local markets. In the short run, however, this is a reminder that food markets are very complex. It is a mistake to assume that every time the price of wheat or corn changes on futures markets, those changes will be immediately and fully reflected in the prices paid to farmers and by consumers around the world.

Final Comment

This appendix is like an introductory survey course in college—it covers a lot of ground, but probably leaves many readers wondering why some topics were covered and others were not. There are many other important questions about world food markets that this appendix and this book do not address. It would be nice to take a longer view of history, for example, to explain how the current system evolved. It would also be good to investigate the public and private decision makers who developed and direct today's world food system. Add a few more topics and we would have the syllabus for Food 201.

Even this rudimentary survey should make it clear how complex the world food system is. In spite of what our kids might think, food does not just come from a grocery store or the local fast food restaurant.

Endnotes

Introduction

1. Bureau of Labor Statistics (BLS) estimates of the consumer price index (CPI) for food. The overall CPI for urban consumers increased at an average rate of 2.7 percent over the same 1991-2006 period, BLS reports.

2. U.S. Department of Agriculture, National Agricultural Statistics Service data. The national average price paid to farmers for corn rose from $1.77 per bushel in November 2005 to $5.47 per bushel in June 2008.

3. U.S. Bureau of Labor Statistics data, available at http://data.bls.gov/PDQ/outside.jsp?survey=cx.

4. FAO press release, "1.02 Billion People Hungry," June 19, 2009, available at www.fao.org/news/story/en/item/20568/icode/. FAO indicates that 915 million were hungry in 2008, and that the 2009 estimate of more than a billion hungry people is based on preliminary information.

5. December 2008 Chicago Board of Trade wheat futures prices declined from $12.84 per bushel on March 13, 2008 to $5.16 on October 24, 2008. December 2008 corn futures fell from $7.96 per bushel on June 27, 2008 to $3.73 on October 24. November 2008 soybean futures dropped from $16.35 per bushel on July 3, 2008 to $8.64 on October 24. Source: DTN.

6. FAO's food price index is reported monthly at www.fao.org/worldfoodsituation/FoodPricesIndex/en/.

7. Donald Mitchell, "A Note on Rising Food Prices." After numerous press reports cited a "secret" World Bank study, the note was formalized and released as a World Bank policy research working paper dated July 2008.

8. The secretary's claim is based on testimony of Edward Lazear, chairman of the President's Council of Economic Advisers, before the Senate Foreign Relations

committee on May 14, 2008. Lazear testified that the increase in corn-based ethanol accounted for just 3 percent of the increase in the International Monetary Fund's Global Food Index over the previous 12 months.

Chapter 1

1. Jean Ziegler, who then served as the U.N. special rapporteur on the right to food, made the charge that diverting cropland to produce biofuels is a "crime against humanity" in a speech at the United Nations (BBC report by Grant Ferrett, October 27, 2007, which can be accessed at http://news.bbc.co.uk/2/hi/americas/7065061.stm).

2. Marketing years begin at the start of the harvest. In the case of U.S. corn, for example, the official 2007/2008 marketing year extends from September 1, 2007 until August 31, 2008. Each crop in each country has its own marketing year, so there are problems with adding up marketing year information.

3. Based on data from the *Sistema Nacional de Información e Integración de Mercados*, a service of Mexico's Economy Secretariat. The average price at the "Centro de Abasto Iztapalapa" increased from 2.25 pesos per kilogram in 2005 to 3.73 pesos per kilogram in 2008, based on author calculations of monthly data.

4. USDA's Economic Research Service, available at www.ers.usda.gov/Briefing/FoodMarketingSystem/.

5. According the Bureau of Labor Statistics reported in September 2009, seasonally adjusted monthly food price inflation was negative in five of the first seven months of 2009.

6. FAO report, "Soaring Food Prices: Facts, Perspectives, Impacts and Actions Required," prepared for the June 2008 "High-Level Conference on World Food Security: The Challenges of Climate Change and Bioenergy," page 28.

7. Based on October 2009 estimates reported in the USDA's World Agricultural Supply and Demand Estimates, the average price received by

U.S. farmers for corn was $4.20 per bushel for the crop harvested in 2007 and $4.06 per bushel for the crop harvested in 2008.

8. USDA, World Agricultural Supply and Demand Estimates, May 2007.

9. Data from USDA's Economic Research Service indicates that Gulf Port corn prices averaged $4.07 per bushel in May 2007 and $7.29 per bushel in June 2008.

10. Hard data on idle plant capacity in 2007 and 2008 is hard to come by, but most plants were operating at or near full capacity until mid-2008.

Chapter 2

1. Source: USDA's Economic Research Service briefing room for farm income and costs, www.ers.usda.gov/Briefing/FarmIncome/, accessed in September 2009. Estimated fuel costs increased by 57 percent, and fertilizer expenses increased by 76 percent between 2005 and 2008.

2. According to the U.N. Food and Agriculture Organization's FAOSTAT database (http://faostat.fao.org/site/575/DesktopDefault.aspx?PageID=575), China and India both used more nitrogen fertilizer between 2002 and 2005 than did the United States. China used an average of 29.2 million metric tons, India used 11.3 million metric tons, and the United States used 11.2 million metric tons. This represents the use of synthetic nitrogen fertilizer, and excludes the nitrogen in livestock manure and other organic fertilizers.

3. This pattern does not hold in many other countries. Corn and wheat yields per acre are more similar in Europe, for example, and so are production costs for the two crops.

4. The per-acre operating costs figures reported in Table 2.1 translate to $1.92 per bushel ($76 per metric ton) for corn and $2.80 per bushel ($103 per metric ton) for wheat. A standard bushel of corn weighs 56 pounds and a standard bushel of wheat weighs 60 pounds.

5. The total area devoted to 13 major crops (corn, soybeans, wheat, upland cotton, sorghum, barley, oats, rice, sunflower seed, peanuts, canola, sugar beets, and sugarcane) increased by about 9 million acres, or about 3.7 percent, between 2005 and 2008, based on USDA reports.

6. Total U.S. fertilizer use increased from 22.1 million tons of active ingredients in 2005 to 22.9 million tons in 2007, based on data from the Economic Research Service of USDA (www.ers.usda.gov/Data/FertilizerUse/, Table 1). Data for 2008 was unavailable.

7. USDA Economic Research Service estimates for 2006, as reported in the appendix.

8. Data from the USDA's Foreign Agricultural Service, "Oilseeds: World Markets and Trade," found at www.fas.usda.gov/psdonline/circulars/oilseeds. pdf. The 2007/2008 average prices were $452 per metric ton in central Illinois and $550 per metric ton in Rotterdam, the Netherlands. For the first eight months of the 2008/2009 marketing year, the Illinois price was $347 per metric ton and the Rotterdam price was $399 per metric ton.

9. Based on data average rural price data from "Datamart Agropecuario," available from the *Servicio de Información Agroalimentaria y Pesquera*, a service of Mexico's Agriculture Secretariat (www.siap.sagarpa.gob.mx/ventana.php?idLiga=1048&tipo=0). Prices are converted to dollars at a 2007 exchange rate of 10.93 pesos per dollar.

10. Author calculations based on Bureau of Labor Statistics data. The seasonally adjusted CPI for food was 200.4 in March 2007 and 213.4 in June 2008.

11. Caroline Saunders and Andrew Barber authored the report, "Comparative Energy and Greenhouse Gas Emissions of New Zealand's and the UK's Dairy Industry." The report is summarized in a press release from Lincoln University in New Zealand, www.lincoln.ac.nz/story21175.html.

12. In 2008, U.S. Energy Information Administration data indicate that U.S. ethanol consumption was about 9.5 billion gallons while total motor gasoline

consumption was about 138 billion gallons. Each gallon of ethanol has approximately two-thirds as many BTUs as a gallon of regular gasoline.

Chapter 3

1. According to the Food and Agriculture Organization's FAOSTAT data set, the world's agricultural population in 2006 was 2.6 billion out of a total world population of 6.6 billion. FAO defines the agricultural population as "all persons depending for their livelihood on agriculture, hunting, fishing, and forestry. It comprises all persons economically active in agriculture as well as their non-working dependents."

2. A good recent book summarizing major agricultural policies and their effects is *A Billion Dollars a Day*, by E. Wesley F. Peterson. West Sussex, UK: Wiley-Blackwell, 2009. For readers who enjoy detailed data and analysis, the Organization for Economic Cooperation and Development issues an annual report, "Agricultural Policies in OECD Countries: Monitoring and Evaluation," which can be found on the OECD website, www.oecd.org.

3. Diouf was quoted in a June 4, 2008 story by Stephanie Holmes of BBC News, "Bioenergy: Fueling the Food Crisis?" Hundreds of other reports and articles could be cited. As reported in Chapter 1, "Biofuel Boom," Jean Ziegler, who then served as the U.N. special rapporteur on the right to food, made the charge that diverting cropland to produce biofuels is a "crime against humanity" in a speech at the United Nations. "The Gallagher Review of the Indirect Effects of Biofuels Production," a July 2008 report by the U.K. Renewable Fuels Agency took a more moderate tone, but recommended a slowdown in the growth of biofuels because of concerns about both the food price and environmental consequences of biofuel production. A July 6, 2008 editorial in the *New York Times* titled "Man-Made Hunger" cited misguided biofuel policies as a major cause of rising food prices.

4. Rapeseed oil prices in Rotterdam, the Netherlands, for example, rose from $660 per metric ton in 2004/2005 to $1,410 per metric ton in 2007/2008. The proportional increases in soybean oil and palm oil prices were even larger.

Source: USDA's Foreign Agricultural Service, "Oilseeds: World Markets and Trade," July 2009.

5. According to USDA's PSD Online, July 2009, E.U. industrial use (primarily for biodiesel) of rapeseed oil grew from 2.6 million metric tons in 2004/2005 to 4.9 million metric tons in 2007/2008. Over the same period, world rapeseed oil use for all purposes increased from 15.5 to 18.4 million metric tons.

6. In the 1985/1986 marketing year, 271 million bushels of corn were used in ethanol plants, and total domestic use of corn was 5,267 million bushels, according to USDA data.

7. It is possible to import ethanol without the $0.54 per gallon tariff if it is imported from countries in the Caribbean and Central America that are provided duty-free access to the U.S. market. Brazilian producers have taken advantage of this provision by shipping partially processed ethanol to eligible countries. These countries complete the processing and ship ethanol to the United States. The amount of ethanol that can be imported duty free is limited to 7 percent of U.S. domestic consumption; actual duty-free imports have been well below this level.

8. According to USDA's September 2009 *World Agricultural Supply and Demand Estimates*, world rice exports in 2007/2008 were 31 million metric tons and world production was 433 million metric tons.

9. September 2009 USDA estimates indicate world rice consumption in 2007/2008 was 428 million metric tons and that world rice stocks rose from 75 million metric tons at the beginning of the year to 80 million metric tons at the end of the year.

10. USDA Foreign Agricultural Service attaché report, "India Grain and Feed Annual, 2009."

11. FAPRI-MU, "Impacts of Selected U.S. Ethanol Policy Options." FAPRI-MU Report #04-09, available at www.fapri.missouri.edu.

12. Net outlays by the two USDA agencies responsible for most U.S. farm programs (the Farm Service Agency and the Risk Management Agency) totaled about $17 billion in fiscal year 2008. USDA spending by program can be found on page 7 of the September 2008 *Monthly Treasury Statement*, available at www.fms.treas.gov/mts/mts0908.pdf.

13. Conservation reserve enrollment estimates are from the USDA Farm Service Agency website, www.fsa.usda.gov. The total area planted to corn, soybeans, wheat, upland cotton, rice, sorghum, barley, oats, sunflowers, peanuts, canola, sugar beets, and sugar cane plus the amount of hay area harvested was 316 million acres, according to June 2009 estimates by USDA's National Agricultural Statistics Service.

Chapter 4

1. *Ending stocks* refers to grain that is left in storage right before the beginning of the following year's harvest. Because each crop in each country has its own production cycle, ending stocks may be measured on different dates across countries and commodities. For example, the U.S. corn harvest begins in September in some southern states, so the official U.S. corn marketing year extends from September 1 until the following August 31. Ending stocks for the 2004/2005 corn marketing year in the United States, therefore, would be the corn that was still in storage on August 31, 2005. Aggregating across the many cereals and countries, ending stocks declined from 585 million metric tons in 1999/2000 to 355 million metric tons in 2003/04, before rebounding to 402 million metric tons at the end of the 2004/05 marketing year, based on USDA PSD data available in September 2009.

2. The long-term trend is computed by a simple linear equation that uses USDA yield data for the 1981–2008 period. Yield is estimated as a function of the calendar year using ordinary least squares. This, of course, ignores a number of arguments about whether the pace of yield growth is changing over time and does not consider prices and other factors that affect production decisions.

3. Quantity data in this section are from USDA's PSD data set, and farm prices are from various publications by USDA's Economic Research Service. U.S. retail food price data are from the Bureau of Labor Statistics.

4. Estimates for the 2008/09 marketing year are preliminary and are based on information from USDA's PSD data set, accessed in September 2009.

5. As in the case of rice, the long-term cereal trend yield is estimated using a very simple linear equation that uses USDA yield data for the 1981–2008 period. Any number of objections could be raised to this simple approach; the only point is to determine whether yields in particular years appear to deviate significantly from the norm. Many factors besides the weather could be responsible for any such deviations.

Chapter 5

1. In 2008, for example, the United States produced 42 million metric tons of beef, pork, chicken, and turkey, plus 86 million metric tons of cow's milk. U.S. livestock and poultry consumed 150 million metric tons of corn alone, and total consumption of grain and oilseed-based feeds amounted to 215 million metric tons. These estimates are author calculations based on USDA reported data for calendar year 2008 (livestock and poultry) and marketing year 2007/2008 (grain and oilseed based feed use).

2. World Bank estimates for China and India available in May 2009 at www.worldbank.org/, under the links to Data and Research. The U.S. growth rate is based on Department of Commerce data.

3. Argentine export prices for soybean oil price averaged $471 per metric ton in 2004/2005 and $1,191 in 2007/2008. Malaysian export prices for palm oil averaged $392 per metric ton in 2004/2005 and $1,058 in 2007/2008. Prices are reported by the USDA Foreign Agricultural Service in its monthly publication, "Oilseeds: World Markets and Trade," May 2009.

4. Income growth estimates by the World Bank and rice consumption estimates from USDA's PSD Online, both from May 2009.

5. USDA's National Agricultural Statistics Service reports the average price paid to farmers fell from $19.40 per hundred pounds in July 2008 to $11.60 in February 2009.

6. USDA's World Agricultural Supply and Demand Estimates, September 2009.

7. USDA's Economic Research Service, "Foreign Agricultural Trade of the United States (FATUS)," May 2009.

8. FATUS, May 2009.

9. Bureau of Labor Statistics data. Preliminary estimates released in September 2009 indicated consumer food price inflation was negative in February, March, April, and May 2009.

10. World Bank estimates of real GDP growth available in May 2009.

11. Lester Brown, *Who Will Feed China? Wake-Up Call for a Small Planet*. New York: W.W. Norton and Company, 1995.

12. Estimates of Chinese and U.S. meat consumption are from USDA's PSD Online data set. Population estimates for 2008 are from FAPRI data sets based on U.S. Census Bureau estimates.

13. Food and Agricultural Policy Research Institute, *FAPRI 2009 U.S. and World Agricultural Outlook*. Ames, Iowa: FAPRI, 2009.

14. USDA's Foreign Agricultural Service, GAIN report number CH9017, March 2009, available at www.fas.usda.gov/gainfiles/200903/146327423.pdf.

15. Based on USDA's PSD Online data set, Chinese and Indian consumption of wheat, rice, and corn increased by 33 million metric tons between 2004/2005 and 2007/2008. World consumption increased by 109 million metric tons, and U.S. use of corn to make ethanol increased by 44 million metric tons.

16. The Center for Disease Control found that 34 percent of adults over the age of 20 were obese in 2005-2006. Source: www.cdc.gov/nchs/pressroom/07newsreleases/obesity.htm.

17. According to the September 2009 World Agricultural Supply and Demand Estimates, total consumption of beef, pork, chicken, and turkey was expected to decline from 216.1 pounds per capita in 2008 to 211.0 in 2009. Final estimates will almost certainly change, but it appears unlikely that the reduction in meat consumption in 2009 will be more than 2 to 3 percent.

18. Bureau of Labor Statistic estimates from May 2009. It would be a mistake to treat these carefully selected observations as definitive evidence of income effects, as monthly prices for various cuts of beef may change for a wide variety of reasons.

19. Estimates are author calculations based on the Department of Commerce's news release on second quarter 2009 GDP, available at www.bea.gov/newsreleases/national/gdp/2009/pdf/gdp2q09_2nd.pdf. The food data is for "food and beverages purchased for off-premises consumption," and the motor vehicle estimates are for "motor vehicles and parts."

Chapter 6

1. Data maintained by USDA's Economic Research Service, available at www.ers.usda.gov/data/feedgrains/StandardReports/YBtable12.htm.

2. All monthly exchange rates used in these examples are from the International Monetary Fund's *International Financial Statistics*, which can be found online at www.imfstatistics.org/imf.

3. September 2009 estimates reported in USDA's PSD Online suggest that Mexico's corn imports in the 2008/2009 marketing year will total about 7.4 million metric tons, down from 8.9 million in 2006/2007 and 9.6 million in 2007/2008. Almost all Mexican corn imports come from the United States.

4. Philip C. Abbott, Christopher Hurt, and Wallace E. Tyner, *What's Driving Food Prices?* Oak Brook, Illinois: Farm Foundation, 2008.

Chapter 7

1. Prices at other locations may be different for a variety of reasons. For example, corn market prices are normally lower in places far from Chicago with surplus corn to sell because of the cost of moving corn from where it is produced to where it is consumed. Likewise, prices are normally higher in places far from Chicago that must import corn from the Midwest. The difference between local cash market prices and futures market prices is referred to as *basis*. As discussed later, the linkages between cash and futures markets are not always as tight as suggested here.

2. Testimony of Michael W. Masters before the U.S. Senate Committee on Homeland Security and Government Affairs, May 20, 2008.

3. U.S. Senate Permanent Subcommittee on Investigations, Committee on Homeland Security and Government Affairs, "Excessive Speculation in the Wheat Market," issued June 24, 2009.

4. The total includes long positions in both futures and options, as reported by the U.S. Commodity Futures Trading Commission in its weekly supplemental commitment of traders report (www.cftc.gov/marketreports/commitmentsoftraders/cot_historical.html).

5. Joachim von Braun and Maximo Torero, "Exploring the Price Spike," *Choices*, 1st quarter 2009. The authors also argue that many of the same fundamental factors discussed in this book were important factors in the increase in food prices.

6. Scott Irwin, "Index Funds and Commodity Prices... Here We Go Again," a guest contribution to *Econbrowser* (www.econbrowser.com/archives/2009/07/guest_contribut.html), July 22, 2009.

7. According to the USDA's PSD Online dataset, September 2009, Chinese corn stocks at the end of the 1999/2000 marketing year were 124 million metric tons and annual consumption that year was 117 million metric tons. By 2007/2008, reported corn stocks had been reduced to 39 million metric tons while consumption had grown to 149 million metric tons.

8. Laura Mandaro, "Credit, Corn Costs Push VeraSun into Chapter 11," *MarketWatch*, November 1, 2008 (www.marketwatch.com/story/verasun-files-for-bankruptcy-after-corn-spiked-credit-tightened).

Chapter 8

1. Estimates from the USDA's PSD Online, August 2009.

2. Just how many hogs died as a result of the disease remains uncertain and controversial, as explained later.

3. Estimates from the USDA's PSD Online, August 2009.

4. According to the USDA's PSD Online, August 2009, imports accounted for less than 1 percent of domestic Chinese pork supplies in 2008. However, the 340,000 metric ton change in Chinese imports between 2006 and 2008 accounted for approximately one-third of the total increase in world pork trade over the same period.

5. Based on the USDA's "Foreign Agricultural Trade of the United States," U.S. pork exports to China and Hong Kong increased by 224,000 metric tons between 2006 and 2008, while total U.S. exports increased by 554,000 metric tons.

6. According to the USDA's PSD Online, August 2009, China feed use of soybean meal increased from 26.9 million metric tons in 2006/2007 to 30.1 million metric tons in 2007/2008.

7. The average price of soybean meal in Decatur, Illinois, increased from $226 per metric ton in 2006/2007 to $370 per metric ton in 2007/2008, according to USDA estimates.

8. All estimates from the USDA's PSD Online, August 2009.

9. A *Washington Post* article by Ariana Eunjung Cha ("Pig Disease in China Worries the World," September 16, 2007) reports Chinese estimates that 2 million pigs fell ill in the summer of 2006 and 400,000 died. The article

reports Chinese government estimates that 68,000 pigs died of the disease in the first eight months of 2007. In contrast, the USDA reports industry estimates that pig deaths numbered in the millions ("The Story Behind China's Rising Pork Prices," Foreign Agricultural Service GAIN Report CH7044).

10. There are some steps farmers and others can take to deal with weather uncertainty, of course. Irrigation is one obvious response to variable rainfall, but is only practical in some areas. Insurance programs can smooth out the effects of weather on farm income, but may do less to reduce volatility in food production and prices. In the long run, of course, efforts to address climate change may have important implications for food markets.

11. World Health Organization, "Bovine Spongiform Encephalopathy," fact sheet released in 2002 and available at www.who.int/mediacentre/factsheets/fs113/en.

12. Per-capita U.S. beef consumption increased from 64.9 to 66.1 pounds, retail weight equivalent, between 2003 and 2004, and average beef retail prices increased from $3.75 to $4.07 per pound, based on USDA data maintained in FAPRI data sets.

13. Estimates from the USDA's PSD Online, August 2009.

14. Alexei Barrionuevo, "Chile Takes Steps to Rehabilitate Its Lucrative Salmon Industry," New York Times, February 4, 2009. Available at www.nytimes.com/2009/02/05/world/americas/05salmon.html.

15. "Gulf's Dead Zone Much Smaller Than Predicted," news story on Physorg.com, July 25, 2009. Available at www.physorg.com/news167720984.html.

16. Based on author calculations of data reported in the USDA's "Sugar and Sweeteners Yearbook Tables," August 2009, per-capita consumption of HFCS decreased from 60.8 pounds in 2005/2006 to 55.7 pounds in 2007/2008, while sugar consumption increased from 69.0 to 70.6 pounds over the same period.

17. No judgment is made about the nutritional consequences of HFCS relative to sugar. According to the American Dietetic Association, "The link

between beverages, HFCS and obesity can largely be accounted for by their contribution to calorie intake." Available on the association's website, www. eatright.org/cps/rde/xchg/ada/hs.xsl/nutrition_7883_ENU_HTML.htm.

18. Lorraine Heller, "'HFCS-free' emerging as new health claim, says Datamonitor," available at www.nutraingredients-usa.com/Consumer-Trends/ HFCS-free-emerging-as-new-health-claim-says-Datamonitor.

Chapter 9

1. United Nations population estimates are from 2008 estimates from the Department of Economic and Social Affairs, available at http://esa.un.org/unpp.

2. In less-developed regions, the reported decline is from 5.9 children per woman in the early 1960s to about 2.7 today. In developed countries, the corresponding decline is from 2.7 to 1.6 children per woman.

3. All of these estimates are from the U.N. population estimates cited above.

4. The United Nations medium variant projection indicates that China's population could peak around 2030 and then actually decline. Between 2010 and 2050, China's projected population increases by just 5 percent, while India's grows by 33 percent and Nigeria's by 83 percent.

5. FAPRI data based on August 2009 information from USDA suggest U.S. per-capita consumption of beef, pork, chicken, and turkey rose from 194 pounds in 1990 to 219 pounds in 2004, before declining to 213 pounds in 2008.

6. For example, Joachim von Braun et al. issued a report in 2008, "International Agricultural Research for Food Security, Poverty Reduction, and the Environment," that summarized research suggesting increased investments in international agricultural research could significantly increase farm productivity and lower food prices. Available at www.ifpri.org/publication/international-agricultural-research-food-security-poverty-reduction-and-environment.

7. Monsanto chairman Hugh Grant, for example, is quoted as saying, "We have committed to using our technology to double yields in our three core crops—corn, soybeans, and cotton—by 2030, while reducing our use of key resources by one-third per unit produced." Grant made the statement at a field event in Iowa on August 13, 2009. Available at http://monsanto.mediaroom.com/index.php?s=43&item=737. If such a goal were met around the world, it would represent more rapid growth in crop yields than experienced in recent decades.

8. See, for example, the U.S. Climate Change Science Program report, "The Effects of Climate Change on Agriculture, Land Resources, Water Resources, and Biodiversity in the United States," available at www.usda.gov/oce/ global_change/files/CCSPFinalReport.pdf.

Appendix

1. 2003 estimates of per-capita food consumption are available at the FAOSTAT section of the FAO website. Crop product estimates are found at http://faostat. fao.org/site/609/default.aspx#ancor, and animal product estimates are at http://faostat.fao.org/site/610/DesktopDefault.aspx?PageID=610#ancor. In September 2009, the FAO website indicated that more current estimates would be available soon.

2. The figures in Table A.2 are calculated by the author based on information in the USDA's PSD Online data set, September 2009. The use figures for oilseeds include the final use of oilseed meals and oils, as well as the direct human and animal consumption of the oilseed. Crush use of oilseeds is excluded to avoid double counting.

3. Silage can be made from corn, hay, and other crops. Grain silage utilizes almost the entire above-ground portion of the plant rather than just the grain. It is suitable for ruminants like cattle, but not for hogs and poultry.

4. Figure A.1 is based on the USDA's PSD data set. Cereals are defined to include corn, wheat, milled rice, barley, sorghum, millet, oats, rye, and mixed grains. Data is on a marketing year basis, where the 2008/2009 marketing year is designated in the chart as 2008. Production data for 2008/2009 generally reflect crops harvested in 2008, while consumption data for 2008/2009 reflects consumption that occurs between the harvests of 2008 and 2009. The September 2009 data is likely to be revised as new information becomes available, especially in the case of the 2007/2008 and 2008/2009 marketing years.

5. U.S. Census Bureau estimates, available at www.census.gov/ipc/www/idb/worldpop.html.

6. The oilseed estimate reflects changes in the production of soybeans, cottonseed, rapeseed, peanuts, and sunflower seed between the 1973–1977 period and the 2003–2007 period. Sugar production increased by 82 percent over that same period. Both the oilseed and sugar data are computed based on the USDA's PSD data set. FAO data from FAOSTAT is used to replace USDA data for soybeans for 1973 to 1977 because of an error in the USDA data.

7. The meat and milk production estimates are from FAOSTAT, http://faostat.fao.org/site/569/default.aspx#ancor.

8. These FAO estimates are from the same FAOSTAT data used in constructing Table A.1.

9. FAO estimates, available at www.fao.org/faostat/foodsecurity/index_en.htm.

10. FAO press release, "1.02 Billion People Hungry," June 19, 2009, available at www.fao.org/news/story/en/item/20568/icode/. FAO indicates that 915 million were hungry in 2008, and that the 2009 estimate of more than a billion hungry people is based on preliminary information.

11. Raj Patel, *Stuffed and Starved: The Hidden Battle for the World Food System*. New York: Melville House Publishing, 2007.

12. Paul Roberts, *The End of Food*. Boston: Houghton Mifflin, 2008.

13. The population figures are calculated based on U.S. Census Bureau estimates. Most of the crop estimates are computed from the USDA's PSD data set. The exception is that FAOSTAT data is used for soybeans for 1973 to 1977, because the USDA data omits Brazilian and Argentine production in those years.

14. Agriculture's share of GDP as reported in a USDA report, "The 20th Century Transformation of U.S. Agriculture and Farm Policy," by Carolyn Dimitri, Anne Effland, and Neil Conklin, available at www.ers.usda.gov/publications/eib3/eib3.htm#changes.

15. FAO defines the agricultural population as "all persons depending for their livelihood on agriculture, hunting, fishing, and forestry. It comprises all persons economically active in agriculture as well as their non-working dependents."

16. The Census of Agriculture reports a wide range of interesting facts about the U.S. farm sector, and is available at www.agcensus.usda.gov.

17. Table 61 of the 2007 Census of Agriculture.

18. Based on USDA estimates in the PSD data set. For example, Cuba generally produces less than 400,000 metric tons of corn in a typical year, but imports (primarily from the United States) have exceeded 500,000 metric tons in every year since 2004/2005, according to USDA.

19. Author calculation based on data included in the USDA's PSD data set.

20. Ibid.

21. Based on data from the Energy Information Administration, March 2009, available at http://tonto.eia.doe.gov/dnav/pet/pet_pnp_oxy_dc_nus_mbbl_a.htm.

22. Author calculations based on data in the USDA's "World Agricultural Supply and Demand Estimates," March 2009 and earlier issues, as well as the PSD data set.

23. USDA's Economic Research Service, available at www.ers.usda.gov/Briefing/CPIFoodAndExpenditures.

24. USDA's Economic Research Service, available at www.ers.usda.gov/data/FarmIncome.

25. USDA's Economic Research Service, available at www.ers.usda.gov/Briefing/FoodMarketingSystem.

26. USDA's Economic Research Service, available at www.ers.usda.gov/Briefing/CPIFoodAndExpenditures.

27. USDA's Economic Research Service, available at www.ers.usda.gov/Data/FarmToConsumer/pricespreads.htm#fruits.

28. UDSA's National Agricultural Statistics Service index of prices received by farmers, available at www.nass.usda.gov/ under "Quick Stats."

29. FAO's "Crop Prospects and Food Situation," April 2009.

Index

A

B